Field Guides to Finding a New Career

Public Safety and Law Enforcement

The Field Guides to Finding a New Career series

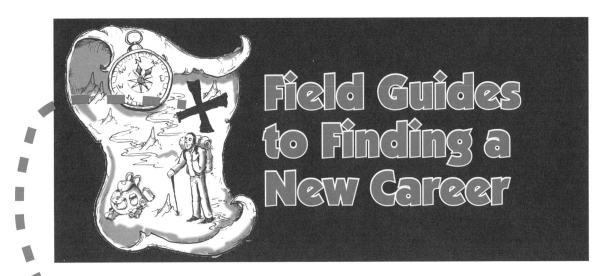

Field Guides
to Finding a
New Career

Public Safety and Law Enforcement

By A. S. Forbes

Ferguson Publishing
An imprint of Infobase Publishing

Field Guides to Finding a New Career: Public Safety and Law Enforcement

Ferguson
An imprint of Infobase Publishing
132 West 31st Street
New York, NY 10001

Library of Congress Cataloging-in-Publication Data

Forbes, A. S.
    Public safety and law enforcement / by Alyson Forbes.
        p. cm. — (Field guides to finding a new career)
    Includes bibliographical references and index.
    ISBN-13: 978-0-8160-8003-8 (hbk. : alk. paper)
    ISBN-10: 0-8160-8003-8 (hbk. : alk. paper)
1. Law enforcement—Vocational guidance—United States—Juvenile literature.
2. Public safety—Vocational guidance—United States—Juvenile literature.
3. Criminal justice, Administration of—Vocational guidance—United States—
Juvenile literature. I. Title.
    HV9950.F65 2009
    363.2023'73—dc22

                                                              2009032832

Ferguson books are available at special discounts when purchased in bulk quantities for businesses, associations, institutions, or sales promotions. Please call our Special Sales Department in New York at (212) 967-8800 or (800) 322-8755.

You can find Ferguson on the World Wide Web at http://www.fergpubco.com

Produced by Print Matters, Inc.
Text design by A Good Thing, Inc.
Illustrations by Molly Crabapple
Cover design by Takeshi Takahashi
Cover printed by Bang Printing, Brainerd, MN
Book printed and bound by Bang Printing, Brainerd, MN
Date printed: March 2010
Printed in the United States of America

10 9 8 7 6 5 4 3 2 1

This book is printed on acid-free paper.

Contents

Introduction: Finding a New Career

Today, changing jobs is an accepted and normal part of life. In fact, according to the Bureau of Labor Statistics, Americans born between 1957 and 1964 held an average of 9.6 jobs from the ages of 18 to 36. The reasons for this are varied: To begin with, people live longer and healthier lives than they did in the past and accordingly have more years of active work life. However, the economy of the twenty-first century is in a state of constant and rapid change, and the workforce of the past does not always meet the needs of the future. Furthermore, fewer and fewer industries provide bonuses such as pensions and retirement health plans, which provide an incentive for staying with the same firm. Other workers experience epiphanies, spiritual growth, or various sorts of personal challenges that lead them to question the paths they have chosen.

Job instability is another prominent factor in the modern workplace. In the last five years, the United States has lost 2.6 *million jobs*; in 2005 alone, 370,000 workers were affected by mass layoffs. Moreover, because of new technology, changing labor markets, ageism, and a host of other factors, many educated, experienced professionals and skilled blue-collar workers have difficulty finding jobs in their former career tracks. Finally—and not just for women—the realities of juggling work and family life, coupled with economic necessity, often force radical revisions of career plans.

No matter how normal or accepted changing careers might be, however, the time of transition can also be a time of anxiety. Faced with the necessity of changing direction in the middle of their journey through life, many find themselves lost. Many career-changers find themselves asking questions such as: Where do I want to go from here? How do I get there? How do I prepare myself for the journey? Thankfully, the Field Guides to Finding a New Career are here to show the way. Using the language and visual style of a travel guide, we show you that reorienting yourself and reapplying your skills and knowledge to a new career is not an uphill slog, but an exciting journey of exploration. No matter whether you are in your twenties or close to retirement age, you can bravely set out to explore new paths and discover new vistas.

Though this series forms an organic whole, each volume is also designed to be a comprehensive, stand-alone, all-in-one guide to getting motivated, getting back on your feet, and getting back to work. We thoroughly discuss common issues such as going back to school, managing your household finances, putting your old skills to work in new situations, and selling yourself to potential employers. Each volume focuses on a broad career field, roughly grouped by Bureau of Labor Statistics' career clusters. Each chapter will focus on a particular career, suggesting new career paths suitable for an individual with that experience and training as well as practical issues involved in seeking and applying for a position.

Many times, the first question career-changers ask is, "Is this new path right for me?" Our self-assessment quiz, coupled with the career compasses at the beginning of each chapter, will help you to match your personal attributes to set you on the right track. Do you possess a storehouse of skilled knowledge? Are you the sort of person who puts others before yourself? Are you methodical and organized? Do you communicate effectively and clearly? Are you good at math? And how do you react to stress? All of these qualities contribute to career success—but they are not equally important in all jobs.

Many career-changers find working for themselves to be more hassle-free and rewarding than working for someone else. However, going at it alone, whether as a self-employed individual or a small-business owner, provides its own special set of challenges. Appendix A, "Going Solo: Starting Your Own Business," is designed to provide answers to many common questions and solutions to everyday problems, from income taxes to accounting to providing health insurance for yourself and your family.

For those who choose to work for someone else, how do you find a job, particularly when you have been out of the labor market for a while? Appendix B, "Outfitting Yourself for Career Success," is designed to answer these questions. It provides not only advice on résumé and self-presentation, but also the latest developments in looking for jobs, such as online resources, headhunters, and placement agencies. Additionally, it recommends how to explain an absence from the workforce to a potential employer.

Changing careers can be stressful, but it can also be a time of exciting personal growth and discovery. We hope that the Field Guides to Finding a New Career not only help you get your bearings in today's employment jungle, but set you on the path to personal fulfillment, happiness, and prosperity.

How to Use This Book

Career Compasses

Each chapter begins with a series of "career compasses" to help you get your bearings and determine if this job is right for you, based on your answers to the self-assessment quiz at the beginning of the book. Does it require a mathematical mindset? Communication skills? Organizational skills? If you're not a "people person," a job requiring you to interact with the public might not be right for you. On the other hand, your organizational skills might be just what are needed in the back office.

Destination

A brief overview, giving you an introduction to the career, briefly explaining what it is, its advantages, why it is so satisfying, its growth potential, and its income potential.

You Are Here

A self-assessment asking you to locate yourself on your journey. Are you working in a related field? Are you working in a field where some skills will transfer? Or are you doing something completely different? In each case, we suggest ways to reapply your skills, gain new ones, and launch yourself on your new career path.

Navigating the Terrain

To help you on your way, we have provided a handy map showing the stages in your journey to a new career. "Navigating the Terrain" will show you the road you need to follow to get where you are going. Since the answers are not the same for everyone and every career, we are sure to show how there are multiple ways to get to the same destination.

Organizing Your Expedition

Fleshing out "Navigating the Terrain," we give explicit directions on how to enter this new career: Decide on a destination, scout the terrain, and decide on a path that is right for you. Of course, the answers are not the same for everyone.

Landmarks

People have different needs at different ages. "Landmarks" presents advice specific to the concerns of each age demographic: early career (twenties), mid-career (thirties to forties), senior employees (fifties) and second-career starters (sixties). We address not only issues such as overcoming age discrimination, but also possible concerns of spouses and families (for instance, paying college tuition with reduced income) and keeping up with new technologies.

Essential Gear

Indispensable tips for career-changers on things such as gearing your résumé to a job in a new field, finding contacts and networking, obtaining further education and training, and how to gain experience in the new field.

Notes from the Field

Sometimes it is useful to consult with those who have gone before for insights and advice. "Notes from the Field" presents interviews with career-changers, presenting motivations and methods that you can identify with.

Further Resources

Finally, we give a list of "expedition outfitters" to provide you with further resources and trade resources.

Make the Most of Your Journey

Public safety is a catch-all term for an incredibly diverse range of careers. Some provide an exhilarating adrenalin rush, others are excellent opportunities for those with a love of the outdoors, and still more are wonderful choices for those getting on in years. What ties them all together, though, is that these careers offer much more than just a paycheck—they offer the opportunity to make a difference in the lives of others.

The people featured in this book—a firefighter from Brooklyn who is carrying on his family's legacy, a police officer who busts methamphetamine labs in the South so that his small hometown might remain a nice place for his kids to grow up, a volleyball coach turned parole officer who thrives helping those in need turn their lives around, and many more—all mention the same thing when asked to sum up why they do these jobs: *I wanted to do something that would allow me to help people and serve my community.* This empathy toward others is the single most important personality trait of anyone successful in these jobs. Another is a desire to work without a strict schedule. Everyone in these careers works in the field. There is little time spent behind a desk. Overtime is the norm. The shifts can be long and arduous. But despite this, the majority of those in these positions are very happy with their work. Why is this? It is because they have a career in which they can make a difference in the lives of those around them.

A word of warning before embarking on the route to one of these careers: quite a few of them are dangerous. One can get injured—possibly seriously—while working in this field. Those considering a career in public safety should take some time for rigorous self-assessment. To be effective in this field, you must be certain that you will not panic when confronted with a perilous situation—that you can rise above any hesitation or fear and just act. Another thing to consider is that a good number of these roles require a level of physical fitness that may be difficult to maintain, specifically firefighters and emergency medical technicians. It is necessary to get into good physical condition and stay committed to it. Otherwise, it will quickly become apparent that, as much as you may desire a career in those fields, your body may not be up to the task.

Most of the careers featured in this book can be placed in one of two categories: those that provide services directly to people in need and those that provide these services indirectly. In the first category are positions such as police officers, firefighters, emergency medical technicians, park rangers, and parole officers. These jobs offer hands-on interaction with the community. Those who want quantifiable evidence of how they are improving the surrounding area would be best served by pursuing one of these roles. In the second category are positions such as information security consultants, private investigators, antiterrorism consultants, forensic science technicians, and building inspectors. These are career paths are for those who prize methodology and detail-oriented work above all else. Most of the work is behind the scenes, and those who do it are rarely applauded publicly. However, their jobs guaranteeing the safety of others are no less vital to the health and well-being of their community.

For the most part, these careers are in fields that are constantly growing, changing, and evolving, and they will continue to offer employment opportunities well into the foreseeable future. Some of the jobs growing most aggressively are those that rely on evolving technology, such as information security and antiterrorism consulting. As law enforcement continues to develop its use of science to fight crime, the field of forensics is becoming more and more specialized. With the boom in real estate development, building inspectors are in demand. There are some careers in this guide that require a bit more tenacity to achieve. Private investigation, firefighting, and park ranger positions are very difficult to find, as they are very attractive to a wide group of people for obvious reasons—there is a romantic appeal to those jobs that may not extend to emergency medical technician, for example. However, those who work in the emergency medical services are more likely to land these more coveted positions down the line. Think about approaching the public safety sector differently than you would any other job. Rather than approaching the position you want directly, it oftentimes pays to sneak in sideways—emergency medical technician to firefighter, or police officer to private investigator. This way, you will get the benefit of added experience, as well as make contacts in the field you ultimately wish to pursue.

The public safety sector has one important distinction from other career paths: many of the positions do not require an advanced education to qualify, although it is often suggested. This makes public safety an accessible line of work for anyone to pursue. It is worth noting, however, that many of these careers have special training and/or certification requirements that may entail some sort of cost to the jobseeker. Some will provide this training through their own academies, such as firefighter and police officer. Still, one should never discount the usefulness of a college degree. It can only enhance your attractiveness to potential employers. With countless opportunities to receive grants, scholarships, and student loans to pay for an education—especially in the adult education realm—there is almost no reason to not pursue higher education. Before electing to skip college and dive right into the working world, investigate the opportunities in your area.

Because the public safety sector is so disparate, a comprehensive overview is almost impossible. This book offers just a glimpse of the many opportunities that abound and is meant as merely an introduction to this ever-changing field. What all of the jobs profiled here have in common is that they will ultimately lead to a much more fulfilling life for yourself and your family. A job you can feel good about is a rare thing and should never be discounted just because it may require some diligence to obtain. The U.S. Bureau of Labor Statistics reports that those who work in the public safety sector often do not receive the six-digit salaries enjoyed by those who work in white-collar office environments, but instead affirm that they feel great about the jobs they do and are grateful to be a part of something bigger than themselves. If you have always wanted to make a difference while making a living, a career in public safety field will ultimately lead to a highly satisfying professional life.

Self-Assessment Quiz

I: Relevant Knowledge

1. How many years of specialized training have you had?
   (a) None, it is not required
   (b) Several weeks to several months of training
   (c) A year-long course or other preparation
   (d) Years of preparation in graduate or professional school, or equivalent job experience

2. Would you consider training to obtain certification or other required credentials?
   (a) No
   (b) Yes, but only if it is legally mandated
   (c) Yes, but only if it is the industry standard
   (d) Yes, if it is helpful (even if not mandatory)

3. In terms of achieving success, how would you rate the following qualities in order from least to most important?
   (a) ability, effort, preparation
   (b) ability, preparation, effort
   (c) preparation, ability, effort
   (d) preparation, effort, ability

4. How would you feel about keeping track of current developments in your field?
   (a) I prefer a field where very little changes
   (b) If there were a trade publication, I would like to keep current with that
   (c) I would be willing to regularly recertify my credentials or learn new systems
   (d) I would be willing to aggressively keep myself up-to-date in a field that changes constantly

5. For whatever reason, you have to train a bright young successor to do your job. How quickly will he or she pick it up?
   (a) Very quickly
   (b) He or she can pick up the necessary skills on the job
   (c) With the necessary training he or she should succeed with hard work and concentration
   (d) There is going to be a long breaking-in period—there is no substitute for experience

II: Caring

1. How would you react to the following statement: "Other people are the most important thing in the world?"
   (a) No! Me first!
   (b) I do not really like other people, but I do make time for them
   (c) Yes, but you have to look out for yourself first
   (d) Yes, to such a degree that I often neglect my own well-being

2. Who of the following is the best role model?
   (a) Ayn Rand
   (b) Napoléon Bonaparte
   (c) Bill Gates
   (d) Florence Nightingale

3. How do you feel about pets?
   (a) I do not like animals at all
   (b) Dogs and cats and such are OK, but not for me
   (c) I have a pet, or I wish I did
   (d) I have several pets, and caring for them occupies significant amounts of my time

4. Which of the following sets of professions seems most appealing to you?
   (a) business leader, lawyer, entrepreneur
   (b) politician, police officer, athletic coach
   (c) teacher, religious leader, counselor
   (d) nurse, firefighter, paramedic

5. How well would you have to know someone to give them $100 in a harsh but not life-threatening circumstance? It would have to be...
   (a) ...a close family member or friend (brother or sister, best friend)
   (b) ...a more distant friend or relation (second cousin, coworkers)
   (c) ...an acquaintance (a coworker, someone from a community organization or church)
   (d) ...a complete stranger

III: Organizational Skills

1. Do you create sub-folders to further categorize the items in your "Pictures" and "Documents" folders on your computer?
   (a) No
   (b) Yes, but I do not use them consistently
   (c) Yes, and I use them consistently
   (d) Yes, and I also do so with my e-mail and music library

2. How do you keep track of your personal finances?
   (a) I do not, and I am never quite sure how much money is in my checking account
   (b) I do not really, but I always check my online banking to make sure I have money
   (c) I am generally very good about budgeting and keeping track of my expenses, but sometimes I make mistakes
   (d) I do things such as meticulously balance my checkbook, fill out Excel spreadsheets of my monthly expenses, and file my receipts

3. Do you systematically order commonly used items in your kitchen?
   (a) My kitchen is a mess
   (b) I can generally find things when I need them
   (c) A place for everything, and everything in its place
   (d) Yes, I rigorously order my kitchen and do things like alphabetize spices and herbal teas

4. How do you do your laundry?
   (a) I cram it in any old way
   (b) I separate whites and colors

    (c)   I separate whites and colors, plus whether it gets dried

    (d)   Not only do I separate whites and colors and drying or non-drying, I organize things by type of clothes or some other system

5. Can you work in clutter?

    (a)   Yes, in fact I feel energized by the mess

    (b)   A little clutter never hurt anyone

    (c)   No, it drives me insane

    (d)   Not only does my workspace need to be neat, so does that of everyone around me

IV: Communication Skills

1. Do people ask you to speak up, not mumble, or repeat yourself?

    (a)   All the time

    (b)   Often

    (c)   Sometimes

    (d)   Never

2. How do you feel about speaking in public?

    (a)   It terrifies me

    (b)   I can give a speech or presentation if I have to, but it is awkward

    (c)   No problem!

    (d)   I frequently give lectures and addresses, and I am very good at it

3. What's the difference between *their, they're,* and *there*?

    (a)   I do not know

    (b)   I know there is a difference, but I make mistakes in usage

    (c)   I know the difference, but I cannot articulate it

    (d)   *Their* is the third-person possessive, *they're* is a contraction for *they are,* and *there is* a deictic adverb meaning "in that place"

4. Do you avoid writing long letters or e-mails because you are ashamed of your spelling, punctuation, and grammatical mistakes?

    (a)   Yes

    (b)   Yes, but I am either trying to improve or just do not care what people think

    (c)   The few mistakes I make are easily overlooked

    (d)   Save for the occasional typo, I do not ever make mistakes in usage

5. Which choice best characterizes the most challenging book you are willing to read in your spare time?

    (a)   I do not read

    (b)   Light fiction reading such as the Harry Potter series, *The Da Vinci Code*, or mass-market paperbacks

    (c)   Literary fiction or mass-market nonfiction such as history or biography

    (d)   Long treatises on technical, academic, or scientific subjects

V: Mathematical Skills

1. Do spreadsheets make you nervous?

    (a)   Yes, and I do not use them at all

    (b)   I can perform some simple tasks, but I feel that I should leave them to people who are better-qualified than myself

    (c)   I feel that I am a better-than-average spreadsheet user

    (d)   My job requires that I be very proficient with them

2. What is the highest level math class you have ever taken?

    (a)   I flunked high-school algebra

    (b)   Trigonometry or pre-calculus

    (c)   College calculus or statistics

    (d)   Advanced college mathematics

3. Would you rather make a presentation in words or using numbers and figures?

    (a)   Definitely in words

    (b)   In words, but I could throw in some simple figures and statistics if I had to

    (c)   I could strike a balance between the two

    (d)   Using numbers as much as possible; they are much more precise

4. Cover the answers below with a sheet of paper, and then solve the following word problem: Mary has been legally able to vote for exactly half her life. Her husband John is three years older than she. Next year,

their son Harvey will be exactly one-quarter of John's age. How old was Mary when Harvey was born?
(a)   I couldn't work out the answer
(b)   25
(c)   26
(d)   27

5.   Cover the answers below with a sheet of paper, and then solve the following word problem: There are seven children on a school bus. Each child has seven book bags. Each bag has seven big cats in it. Each cat has seven kittens. How many legs are there on the bus?
(a)   I couldn't work out the answer
(b)   2,415
(c)   16,821
(d)   10,990

VI: Ability to Manage Stress

1.   It is the end of the working day, you have 20 minutes to finish an hour-long job, and you are scheduled to pick up your children. Your supervisor asks you why you are not finished. You:
(a)   Have a panic attack
(b)   Frantically redouble your efforts
(c)   Calmly tell her you need more time, make arrangements to have someone else pick up the kids, and work on the project past closing time
(d)   Calmly tell her that you need more time to do it right and that you have to leave, or ask if you can release this flawed version tonight

2.   When you are stressed, do you tend to:
(a)   Feel helpless, develop tightness in your chest, break out in cold sweats, or have other extreme, debilitating physiological symptoms?
(b)   Get irritable and develop a hair-trigger temper, drink too much, obsess over the problem, or exhibit other "normal" signs of stress?
(c)   Try to relax, keep your cool, and act as if there is no problem
(d)   Take deep, cleansing breaths and actively try to overcome the feelings of stress

3. The last time I was so angry or frazzled that I lost my composure was:
    (a) Last week or more recently
    (b) Last month
    (c) Over a year ago
    (d) So long ago I cannot remember

4. Which of the following describes you?
    (a) Stress is a major disruption in my life, people have spoken to me about my anger management issues, or I am on medication for my anxiety and stress
    (b) I get anxious and stressed out easily
    (c) Sometimes life can be a challenge, but you have to climb that mountain!
    (d) I am generally easygoing

5. What is your ideal vacation?
    (a) I do not take vacations; I feel my work life is too demanding
    (b) I would just like to be alone, with no one bothering me
    (c) I would like to do something not too demanding, like a cruise, with friends and family
    (d) I am an adventurer; I want to do exciting (or even dangerous) things and visit foreign lands

Scoring:

For each category...

For every answer of *a*, add zero points to your score.
For every answer of *b*, add ten points to your score.
For every answer of *c*, add fifteen points to your score.
For every answer of *d*, add twenty points to your score.

The result is your percentage in that category.

Field Guides to Finding a New Career

Public Safety and Law Enforcement

Police Officer

Police Officer

Career Compasses

Guide yourself to a career as a police officer.

 **Relevant knowledge** of law enforcement practices, as well as county, state, and federal regulations (30%)

 **Ability to Manage Stress** to cope with possibly dangerous situations with criminal offenders (30%)

 **Communication Skills** to effectively question suspects and write up in-depth police reports (20%)

 **Organizational Skills** to handle a large number of cases at one time (20%)

Destination: Police Officer

 On a radio show recently, a veteran police officer spoke about a time he responded to a car accident in which a van had slid to a halt on someone's front lawn. As he interviews the driver, who is holding the hand of his pet chimpanzee, he learns that this chimpanzee became agitated while the pair were driving home, grabbed the steering wheel away from the driver, and subsequently crashed the van. The driver is adamant that he is not at fault. The chimpanzee is frightened. The cop is confused. The

lawn is a mess. And the whole scenario does much to convey the single most important challenge any police officer faces—working without precedent. Police officers learn quickly that when they are forced off of the map, they need to be fast-thinking enough to find a way home.

Most people who seek employment as police officers fall into three categories: the first group has an interest in helping people and the community, the second group craves a job that will get the adrenalin pumping, and the third group watches all the police procedurals and wants a cool job like the actors on television. The best police officers tend to be a mix of the first two. Those who fall into the third category should be warned: what is portrayed on television is often very different than a law enforcement career in reality. If the producers aired a show that portrayed law enforcement as it really is, you may watch a few hours of a police officer sitting at a desk filling out traffic reports, not a high-energy police pursuit filled with gunfire and exploding cars.

This is not to downplay the element of danger that exists in the life of a police officer. Confrontations with criminals—whether armed or not—can be highly stressful and require a level head, as well as a dash of old-fashioned bravery. Law enforcement officers are often in the presence of death and dying through accidents or homicide, sometimes delivering the news of a person's passing to relatives. Being a member of a police force in a high-crime area can take a toll on the officer's family, as they must face the possibility of a loved one being injured or even killed while on shift. Also, despite being scheduled for a regular workweek, most work overtime during investigations and are constantly on call. Even an off-duty police officer can be armed and, if privy to a crime being committed, is required to act.

Essential Gear

An eagle eye. Police officers are always on the look out for not only crimes in progress, but also crimes that have not yet happened. Suspicious individuals, unsafe conditions, or situations that just do not feel right are ripe for investigation. Detectives involved in isolating and interpreting a crime scene may need to spot the proverbial needle in the haystack. The soda can placed slightly away from the others could harbor DNA evidence of the last person to leave the scene. The placement of clothing on a floor can indicate whether or not a victim knew their attacker. It is important to learn how to take in and interpret these clues—and more importantly, know that they are there in the first place.

The most important duty of a police officer is to protect the lives and property of the citizens within their jurisdiction. This requires the pursuit and apprehension of those who break the law and threaten the peace of a community. The range of crimes falling within that loose definition is astounding. A police officer could go from issuing a citation for disturbing the peace to a man who is feeling a little boisterous while walking home late at night to investigating a double murder just a few blocks away a half an hour later. Large police departments typically sort their officers into various squads, all of which are responsible for a specific type of crime—homicide, robbery, narcotics, traffic, K-9, and more.

Essential Gear

Personal integrity. A person looks to the police to ensure personal safety and the safety of their families. It is important that a police officer project an air of honesty, responsibility, and integrity. The specter of the rogue cop, popularized in movies like *Serpico, Witness,* and *L.A. Confidential,* looms large in the heads of many would-be police officers, but it is not the norm by any stretch of the imagination. Instead, police officers should be the public face of the community, friendly, non-threatening, and excellent in public meetings and situations.

With this positioning, police officers are much more attuned to the type of crime they are responsible for investigating, which will in turn lead to higher "solve" rates.

Although many aspiring police officers envision themselves working within a local police department, there is actually a wealth of opportunities at the federal level. The Federal Bureau of Investigation (FBI) employs scores of agents that conduct national security investigations, such as organized crime, kidnapping, white-collar crimes such as embezzlement and bank fraud, drug trafficking, and terror threats. The U.S. Drug Enforcement Agency (DEA) investigate crimes specific to illegal drugs. The Bureau of Alcohol, Tobacco, Firearms, and Explosives (ATF) mainly deal with enforcing laws governing firearms. The Department of Homeland Security fights the nation's battle against terrorism. Other possibilities for a law enforcement career on the federal level exist within U.S. Border Patrol, the Federal Air Marshals, and the Secret Service; or as an immigration inspector, customs inspector, or U.S. Marshal.

However, should this career path lead to a position with a police precinct, a police officer has quite a bit of room for growth and specialization. The entry-level position is patrolman. Patrolmen can expect to spend a lot of time walking or driving through their assigned neighborhoods, acting as a deterrent to crime with police presence, or working to apprehend criminals and enforce traffic laws. Police officers can expect to become eligible for advancement after six months to three years of patrol work. After this probationary period, qualified police officers can expect to either be promoted to detective—which allows the officer to pursue and solve long-term investigations—or to specialize in one type of police work, such as juvenile offenders. To reach the rank of corporal, sergeant, captain, sergeant, lieutenant, and captain, officers must score highly on a written test and have exemplary on-the-job performance. In some counties, the position of sheriff is also available, but one must be elected by the community to the office.

The salary of a police officer is not extraordinarily high, but it is enough to allow for a comfortable middle-class existence, and gracious pension plans allow many police officers to retire after 25 years of service. But the pay is secondary to the work for most police officers. They feel a calling to the work, no matter what the compensation. As Keith Weaver, an investigator in Clarendon, Arkansas, said about why he chose to pursue a career in law enforcement, "I cannot give one good reason. I ask myself that same question on occasion. But I do know that the best part is feeling that I can make a real difference in people's lives, that there is more to the job than just putting the 'bad guys' in jail." Every police officer would agree.

You Are Here

Set yourself on the path to becoming a police officer.

Do you keep a cool head under pressure? Think about these three scenarios: First, while making a routine traffic stop, the driver of the car seems nervous and volatile. He will not show you his hands, nor respond to your request that he step out of the car. Second, you arrive at a call to discover a man standing on the roof of a building. With each step you make toward him, he inches closer to the edge, threatening to jump if you come any closer. Third, a neighborhood resident is concerned about the presence of a group of adolescents congregating in a nearby playground. They are noisy and act out in an abusive manner. You arrive at the playground and they begin threatening you when you ask them to move along.

These three set-ups are very common occurrences in the life of a police officer, especially a first responder who may have to approach a scene alone until back up arrives. In each of these scenarios, it sounds tempting to use force in order to obtain compliance. However, force should only be used sparingly, if at all. You must instead be a facilitator. Police officers are masters of convincing others that their orders are to be followed without betraying any signs of weakness—and smart enough to figure out the best approach to doing so without anyone getting hurt.

Does methodical work appeal to you? Many police officers, especially detectives, find themselves a part of long-term investigations. From the moment they step into a crime scene, they are responsible for collecting evidence, taking witness statements—many of which may not correlate with one another—pursuing leads, and bringing in suspects. Once a suspect is identified, the assigned officer is responsible for interrogation and—hopefully—obtaining a confession. That officer is then expected to testify in court and provide any evidence needed to make sure that the suspect is convicted and forced to make reparations for the crime. Depending on the situation, this process can take a few days, weeks, or months. Some particularly difficult cases can take many years. A police officer must remain focused on achieving closure for a victim and their family, no matter how cold a case may become.

Would you consider yourself a dedicated individual? The median pay for a patrol officer is approximately $47,000 per year. Needless to say, those who choose to pursue this career path do not do so with an eye on becoming a millionaire. Instead, you will often hear stories like, "My father is a police officer and I wanted to follow in his footsteps," or, "A police officer impacted my life in a positive way and I really wanted to make the same difference in another's life." A career in law enforcement is a calling. In the face of danger, police officers must focus on a positive outcome. If offered a bribe, one must be dedicated to upholding the police creed to protect and serve in a way that benefits the community. You may be an unsung hero, but knowing that each day on patrol is a day that you are making everyone a little safer must be compensation enough.

Navigating the Terrain

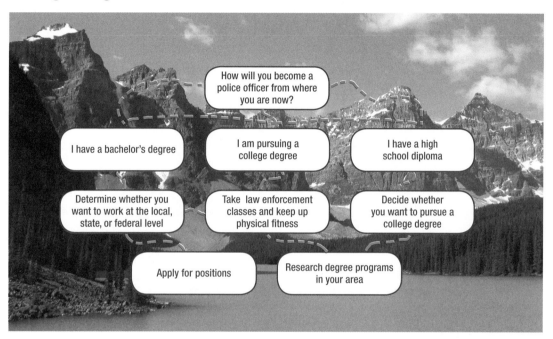

How will you become a
police officer from where
you are now?

I have a bachelor's degree

I am pursuing a
college degree

I have a high
school diploma

Determine whether you
want to work at the local,
state, or federal level

Take law enforcement
classes and keep up
physical fitness

Decide whether
you want to pursue a
college degree

Apply for positions

Research degree programs
in your area

Organizing Your Expedition

Get everything in order as you prepare to become a police officer.

Decide on a destination. Although you can conceivably become a police officer directly after graduating from high school, most police departments prefer that any applicant have some secondary educational experience. Aspiring police officers not wishing to pursue a bachelor's degree often take a few classes in criminal justice and police science in preparation for the entrance exam. Another option for those who decide on law enforcement as a career early in life is to become a police cadet. These cadets are generally confined to office work, but attend classes until they meet the age requirement to enlist. Finally, a good preliminary practice is to join a sports team or club. This encourages physical fitness and stamina, as well as the importance of cooperation and solidarity—all excellent traits that are heavily sought after in applicants to the police force.

Notes from the Field

Keith Weaver
Investigator, First Judicial District Drug Task Force
Clarendon, Arkansas

What were you doing before you decided to become a police officer?

Before getting into law enforcement I worked in my family's retail furniture business and did part-time work as a firefighter and an emergency medical technician.

What was involved in terms of education and training?

In Arkansas, it is standard for a full-time certified law enforcement officer to spend twelve weeks in the Arkansas Law Enforcement Training Academy. Independently, I then chose to continue my education with courses offered by the University of Arkansas and other agencies. However, I have always found it odd that the only profession that by law gives a person the right to take the life of another human being does not actually require continuing education to maintain your certification.

Scout the terrain. Everyone pursuing a career in law enforcement must determine where he or she most wants to work. If a federal level position is desired, the applicant must be a college graduate and have at least three years of employment experience in a related field. Useful degrees include accounting, engineering, information technology, or computer science, as well as law or criminal justice. Federal-level police officers must also be fluent in a foreign language. Because of these restrictions, any aspiring applicant must determine at the onset if further education is needed. After reviewing the requirements of a career path on the federal level, many happily pursue a career with a local police precinct to avoid the expense and time necessary in attaining advanced degrees and training.

Find the path that's right for you. After passing an entrance exam, physical fitness test, and a drug screening, most police recruits are then required to attend the police academy before they can be assigned a full-time post with their department. This academy training is generally 12 to 14 weeks long. During these weeks, cadets will receive lessons in constitutional law and civil rights, regional laws and restrictions, and

What are the keys to success and the qualities of a good police officer?

Twenty years ago, I would have said street smarts, guts, and a willing-ness to knock the heck out of someone. A police officer now finds that he/she must be a lawyer, doctor, counselor, minister, computer technician, and mother/father figure. But most of all, a good police officer must have thick skin—police officers find themselves in the unique position of being hated until we are needed, and then being criticized that we are not doing our job correctly. I think of it this way: a good police officer is like someone in the ministry—the job is a calling.

What surprised you the most about your role as a police officer?

What surprised me the most is just how much crime is outside every-one's front door. When a citizen looks out the window, they will see the green grass, flowers, and birds, but when a police officer looks outside we see the crack dealer, thief, rapist, and murderer—the world will never look the same once you become a police officer.

accident and criminal investigation. They will also train in the use of firearms and self-defense, as well as emergency response and general first-aid. They will sometimes be summoned to help with ongoing investigations by going door-to-door seeking witnesses, or combing large crime scenes for evidence. During this time in the police academy, most recruits begin to formulate a career plan for themselves through the discovery of what type of criminal investigation appeals to them the most. Once they graduate and are assigned as patrol officers, they can then work to achieve the placements and promotions that best fit their interests to create the most fulfilling career.

Landmarks

If you are in your twenties . . . The majority of police officers begin training in their early twenties, entering the law enforcement field after receiving a criminal justice college degree. However, a college education is not necessary to be successful in police work, and anyone who is sharp-thinking, displays good communication skills, and is in good physical condition should find the entrance exam and accompanying fitness tests relatively straightforward.

If you are in your thirties or forties . . . Many men and women who have been in the military find employment within police forces when they are discharged. This type of experience can be helpful in finding employment in the more specialized fields of federal law enforcement.

If you are in your fifties . . . Patrol work requires a high level of physical fitness. However, if you have prior experience working in some type of law enforcement, it is not impossible to obtain work as a police officer at a later stage in life. Look for large police departments that have more office-based opportunities available, such as maintaining the evidence room, or staff supervisory positions.

If you are over sixty . . . Have you been working in the law enforcement field? If so, in many counties the position of sheriff is a natural fit for a person who is a respected public servant. Because it is an elected office, it will be necessary to campaign for the post. If you have years of experience working within your community, it can be fairly easy to run a successful campaign, especially in rural or sparsely populated areas.

Further Resources

Discover Policing is a comprehensive Web site for anyone interested in becoming a police officer, either as a first career, or as a career change, as well as personal stories from those who are new to the law enforcement field. http://discoverpolicing.org

The **International Association of Chiefs of Police** is the oldest non-profit association of police executives in the world. http://www.theiacp .org

The **National Law Enforcement Recruiters Association (NLERA)** tracks federal, state, and local law enforcement job fairs, recruiting events, and other career opportunities throughout the United States. http://www.nlera.org

Officer.com is an online resource for all things police-related, including new technologies, noteworthy news stories, and nationwide employment listings. http://www.officer.com

Information Security Consultant

Information Security Consultant

Career Compasses

Guide yourself to a career as an information security consultant.

Relevant knowledge of the networking systems that must be secured (40%)

Communication Skills to educate and train staff to follow new security procedures, as well as explain difficult security concepts to colleagues (30%)

Organizational Skills to determine what security measures need to be put in place (20%)

Mathematical Skills to understand computing and networking as a whole (10%)

Destination: Information Security Consultant

When business was conducted with a pen and paper, anyone who wished to steal a company's secrets had to physically break down the door and roll the filing cabinet away. Now that computers and their information systems have long become the norm, it is possible to compromise a company's network and make off with anything—credit card information, proprietary secrets, employee information, and more—all without entering the building, or even being in the same hemisphere. Any network that transmits information is vulnerable, and information security consultants are there to help protect this information and keep it safe.

As the use of electronic or Internet-based data processing continues to expand, all organizations have recognized the need to better protect the information that is being stored, processed, or transmitted through the company and to their clients. Most large corporations, universities, or hospitals tend to have a staff member who acts as the information security officer (ISO) and maintains the integrity of their computer networks on a permanent basis. However, it can be more lucrative to work as a consultant—that is, move from company to company as needed. In this role, many information security consultants are called in specifically to help coordinate the development of an information security system or comprehensive privacy program.

Essential Gear

A thumb drive. Sometimes called a flash drive, this tiny portable hard drive is any information security consultant's friend. Small enough to hook onto a key chain, these storage devices have plenty of space to hold all your security tools and applications and can be easily plugged into any computer with a USB port.

The basic principle of information security is known as the CIA triad—confidentiality, integrity, and availability. It is the responsibility of an information security consultant to evaluate the core structure of any organization, determine what information is most sensitive, and develop a plan that guarantees that those three concepts are met within the network they are working to safeguard. Confidentiality refers to preventing the disclosure of information to unauthorized parties. This could mean anything from an employee revealing a computer password to another person inadvertently to making sure credit card numbers that pass through an e-commerce site are encrypted. Hospitals, banks, payroll processing centers, law offices, government offices, or other organizations that handle large amounts of personal data are required by law to protect this information from all outside parties to prevent identity theft, corporate espionage, and other crimes caused by breaches of confidentiality. In the world of information security, integrity means that all employees of a company work to protect their employers' information. Information security personnel create devices that prevent errors of integrity, such as an employee sending an e-mail in error that contains sensitive information. Finally, an information security consultant must make information available to those that require it in order to do their job effectively by preventing service interruptions and checking to make sure the system networks are online as consistently as possible, and by hindering "denial of service attacks"—a person or virus that interrupts the workings of a network or Web site with intent to harm.

When setting up a new information security system, the first thing that any consultant would want to do is assess what is most important to the inner workings of an organization and develop a risk management plan—in simple terms, figure out what terrible things could happen to that organization's network due to vulnerabilities or outside threats, and how to best prevent them. To select what needs improvement, information security consultants will look at the following things: the network's organization, the security of the human resources department, the way that information is acquired and stored within the databases, the people who currently have access to this information, and the security policy that is in place and how well the organization is adhering to it. Once a plan has been forged, the information security consultant will implement it.

Essential Gear

A smart phone. Any consultant in any field will admit that in order to keep the jobs coming, it is necessary to be reachable at any time. Invest in a Blackberry or other so-called smart phone. This way you can receive not only calls, text messages, and e-mails while out of the office, but you can also remotely link into your organization's network and troubleshoot if need be—all from the comfort of your sofa.

The new security plan should have at least three levels, or controls. The first is administrative. This involves educating employees about any new procedures, setting new passwords, and working to enforce disciplinary action against those who are responsible for breaching security. Secondly, information security consultants will work on the logical controls—the software that will control access to the computer networks. Computer security works best when the "principle of least privilege" is imposed. Employees are classified and granted information based on that classification—an employee has only the information that he or she needs to do the job at hand. Lastly, physical controls are the actual barriers that are placed between the outside world and the information contained within a company's walls.

Once this new security plan has been implemented, the information security consultant works to maintain its integrity, troubleshoot any problems that arise, defend against outside attacks, and continually inspect the network for any security breaches. With the popularity of cyber attacks, many information security consultants will test their networks with security audits like penetration testing, where the consultant intentionally attacks their own networks in the hope of detecting any flaws.

Demand for information security consultants will only grow as organizations—and those who wish to abscond with the data housed within them—become savvier. In fact, it is projected that the field of computer support specialists will grow by more than 18 percent in the next 10 years. Those interested in pursuing this field will be best served by obtaining at least a bachelor's degree in computer science, information technology, or information security. However, it is not unusual for information security consultants to be self-trained. The transition to information security can be made even more effortless for those with a background in information technology. The field of information security is constantly evolving, and it is sure to be a successful career path as computers remain an essential component of everyday life and commerce.

You Are Here

Set yourself on the path to becoming an information security consultant.

Do you have strong analytical skills? The role of an information security consultant is primarily that of a problem-solver. Once the new security plan has been put into place, an information security consultant must spend anywhere from a few weeks to a few months testing the integrity of the system. If a problem is found, it is the consultant who must find a way to make a repair, or revamp the system to provide the needed security. Consultants also work for organizations of varying sizes. A small nonprofit must secure their data, yet will not be able to afford the elaborate computer networking and security software an international banking conglomerate may have. As a consultant, it is important to supply the same level of service—and the same level of security—no matter what standard of equipment is available.

Do you have a high level of personal integrity? Information security consultants often have access to the personal data of an entire organization. Obviously, they must never be tempted to compromise this information for their own gain. This requires that information security consultants be honorable, reliable, and discreet at all times, even more so if a consultant is working for a company that houses highly sensitive proprietary data sought after by another organizations in that industry.

Do you keep abreast with new technology? Computer technology is constantly advancing. A successful information security consultant must stay current. Because working as a consultant means working for yourself, the responsibility of ongoing education falls to you. Subscribe to trade journals for the field of information technology. Invest in computer classes to learn new software, as well as to investigate new security tactics as they become available. Check the further resources listed at the end of this chapter. Many of these industry organizations list workshops and seminars for information security specialists throughout the United States. As a consultant, these business expenses will be tax deductions—even more of a reason to follow through with them!

Navigating the Terrain

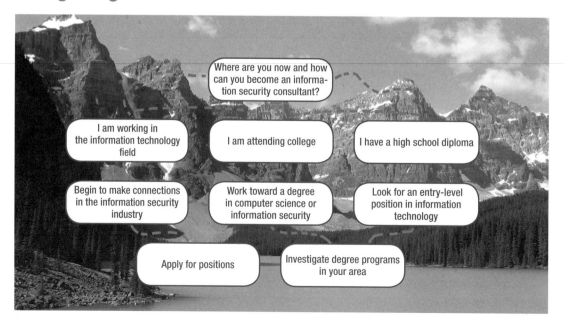

Organizing Your Expedition

Get everything in order as you prepare to become an information security consultant.

Decide on a destination. Many information security consultants are self-taught. They may have spent many years working in information technology or computer science and slowly evolved into security specialists. However, today's organization often looks to a college degree to ensure that those working to protect their data are fully trained in their field. Most colleges offer computer science degrees, but if a career path in information security is desired, it may be best to study for a degree in information security specifically. Those who are already educated or working in a computer-related field may be best served by attending an intensive course in information security rather than completing another degree.

Scout the terrain. Those that aspire to work in the field of information security often begin by obtaining a full-time position with the information technology department of an organization. Entry-level positions in IT are more readily available, especially to those whose talent with a computer is self-taught. While working in that field, begin to make contacts with outside consultants within the information security sector. It is possible that these consultants may be seeking someone to assist in making contact with potential clients, or helping to run security audits. This is a wonderful way to learn information security from the inside out, and this knowledge can then be applied to soliciting an exclusive client-base once aspiring consultants are ready to strike out on their own.

Find the path that's right for you. Working as a consultant means marketing yourself to prospective clients. To begin gathering a client base, a consultant should first determine what level of training he or she must reach in order to present themselves as fully qualified for the job at hand. The GIAC-GSEC and Security+ are the lowest level certifications that an information security consultant should hold. From there, a consultant can choose to move on to the Certified Information Systems Security Professional (CISSP) certification. There are also four other advanced certificates an information security consultant can hope to attain. These are the Information Systems Security Architecture Professional (ISSAP), Information Systems Security Engineering Professional (ISSEP), Infor-

Notes from the Field
Kurt Seifried
Information security analyst
Edmonton, Alberta, Canada

What were you doing before you decided to become an information security consultant?

I am not even sure I really ever consciously decided to be an information security consultant until well past it happening. I do remember consciously deciding to share the information I found and learned about Linux security in the form of the *Linux Administrator Security Guide* (LASG) many years ago, because I figured if this was as much of a problem for me as for other people they wouldd appreciate having it written down so they would not have to re-discover the wheel, so to speak. I also remember consciously realizing, "If I can connect to the Internet, that means people can connect to me and my machine."

Why did you decide to pursue a career as an information security consultant?

Again, this sort of fell into my lap. Jim Reavis, then at SecurityPortal, needed some contract work done (a selection of security software related to a book), which I did for them. He then offered me a contract position writing for SecurityPortal and it just sort of grew steadily from there.

What was involved in terms of education and training?

I am largely self-taught. The availability of Open Source (Linux, Apache, Sendmail, etc) not only let me examine the inner workings, but it was

mation Systems Security Management Professional (ISSMP), and Certified Information Security Manager (CISM). These certificates indicate that the consultant is trained in specific topics within information security: information security architecture, engineering, and management. Those with superior certification levels will appear most appealing to a prospective client. Also, most computer system or networking manufacturers, such as Microsoft or Cisco Systems, offer their own certifications that may be worth looking into should a consultant wish to specialize.

also free as in free beer, which is important if you are a seventeen-year-old high school student (who probably does not have the cash on hand to buy a commercially licensed UNIX). I can only see as far as I can because I am lucky enough to stand on the shoulder of giants (Torvalds, Stallman, etc). I was also lucky that my dad was willing to drop some serious money on a 486DX2/66 with eight megabytes of RAM, which had the advantage of being able to compile stuff relatively quickly.

What are the keys to success and the qualities of a good information security consultant?

Curiosity and the willingness to verify how the system works (it might not behave the way it claims to). The ability to understand complex systems with pieces that you may not be able to directly examine or understand is also crucial. The ability to read, source code, man pages, Web pages, etc. There is literally a ton of information out there, but much of it is not written to be highly accessible (one reason I did the LASG).

What surprised you the most about your role as an information security consultant?

How much it changes and also how little it changes. On the one hand we are starting to become more professional (certifications, efforts like CWE, CVE, etc) and on the other hand we are still largely in the dark ages (security solutions are handcrafted by artisans). I think what surprises me most is that information security has not really been well integrated with risk management on the business side. It is still seen as a necessary evil, as opposed to something that is well accepted.

Landmarks

If you are in your twenties . . . If you have no previous knowledge of information technology, it will be best to pursue a degree in information security specifically, especially if you know that the career path you would like to follow. Research schools in your area that offer this major. Information security is a very serious matter to organizations, and a bachelor's degree will lend gravity to your résumé when you begin seeking work.

If you are in your thirties or forties . . . If you have been working in information technology, brush up on what computer skills you have with a few classes or seminars in information security. This way, while soliciting business for yourself, you will be able to impress upon your prospective clients that you have thorough knowledge of the latest advances in the field.

If you are in your fifties . . . A computer hobbyist can easily transition into information technology, and then on to security. Turn the knowledge you gained at home into an entry-level placement with an information technology firm or department. Once you learn the ins and outs of corporate information technology support, you can begin to move into consulting for the information security sector.

If you are over sixty . . . It is never too late to pursue a career in information security, especially if you are already working in a computer technology trade. If your training is up to date, begin by refocusing your résumé to reflect any experience with information security. As a consultant, your age (and wisdom) will be seen as a positive.

Further Resources

The **Federal Trade Commission** has made available a free online tutorial in information security for businesses. It is a solid overview of what steps an organization—and their information security consultant—should be taking to protect the integrity of their information. http://www.ftc.gov/infosecurity

The **League of Professional System Administrators** is a nonprofit corporation that works to support system administrators and other technology professionals through education and outreach, employment listings, and message board discussions with topics such as up-to-date information sharing of information security tactics. http://lopsa.org

The **National Workforce Center for Emerging Technologies** offers innovative information technology workshops, seminars, and longer educational programs, as well as educational products on information management. http://www.nwcet.org

Private Investigator

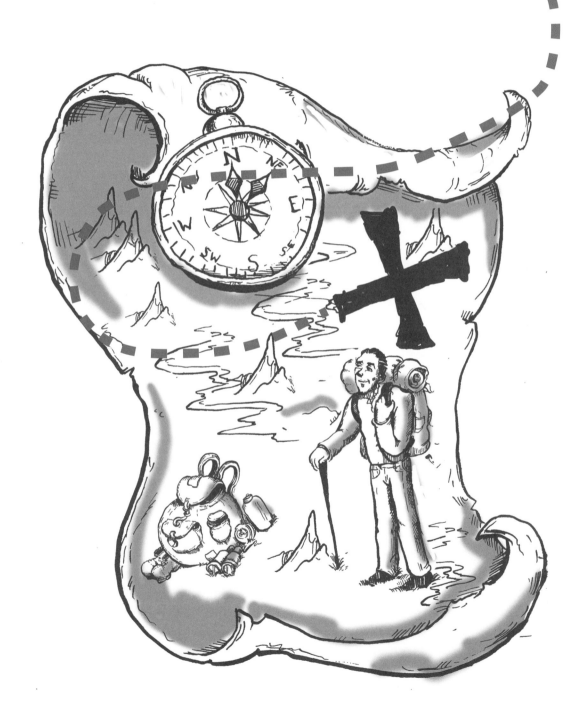

Private Investigator

Career Compasses

Guide yourself to a career as a private investigator.

Communication Skills to conduct effective interviews, determine the best questions to ask, detect when information is being withheld, provide information to your clients clearly and concisely, and effectively testify in court trials (40%)

Organizational Skills to maintain files of information and best determine what information is most useful (30%)

Relevant Knowledge of the investigative tools at your disposal in order to understand how to gather evidence in a way that uses your time effectively (20%)

Ability to Manage Stress to cope with irregular hours and the possibility of confrontation (10%)

Destination: Private Investigator

The term *private investigator* conjures up a very striking image for most people: the mysterious figure in a trench coat and fedora, standing on a rainy city street with a camera raised to one eye, or parked at a heavy oak desk behind a stenciled, smoked glass door. Writers all around the world have made their fortunes writing about these very characters. Luckily, it is not too far from the truth. But the aspects that paint that romantic picture of private investigation can actually be the most grueling qualities of a particular case, and the work that is not featured in the pages of our favorite Sam Spade novels can be some of the most engaging.

Explained in its most simplistic form, a private investigator is hired by an individual, business, or law firm to gather information. The type of investigation that is undertaken is usually referred to as a "physical investigation." One of the most stereotypical examples of this type of case offers a comprehensive overview. A wife believes that her husband has strayed. A detective may be engaged to conduct an investigation. First, the investigator will gain access to a subject's computer and attempt to retrieve incriminating e-mails or documents. Next, bank account or credit card statements may be pulled and suspicious charges will be checked. Then, a detective may telephone or approach the friends or coworkers of the subject to see if any information can be gained in that way. If these routes do not lead to a confirmation of an affair, perhaps the investigator will trail the subject over the course of a few days to determine a daily routine and undertake surveillance: using photographic or video equipment, the investigator may observe the subject's workplace, home, or covertly follow the subject's movements until it is possible to confirm or deny the existence of a mistress. If there is indeed something to report, it falls to the investigator to break the news to his employer, as well as introduce the evidence gathered. Often, this is the most difficult aspect of a case; it is never clear how a distraught client will react once they receive the answers they were looking for.

Essential Gear

Make friends—with everybody. The single most powerful tool a detective can have is an extensive network of contacts. Many investigators actively seek out those in government or law enforcement positions that can provide information that may not be available to the general public. Some rely on their former co-workers on the police force, a sister-in-law that works at the department of motor vehicles, or an old college buddy that writes for the newspaper. But if you are not so well connected going into your career as a detective, all is not lost. Become a regular at a local cop hangout, attend city council meetings, or join the Lion's Club. Once you begin moving in the same circles as the contacts you want to cultivate, it is only a matter of time before you make some friends in high places. One detective mentioned that she keeps an address book specifically for her investigative work—whenever she meets someone who could potentially be a help to her, no matter how briefly, the name and number goes right in the book.

In addition to this, detectives also carry out background profiles for private citizens, pre-employment verification, or premarital screening; assist in criminal or civil liability cases, especially in realm of child custody and protection; investigate suspect insurance or workers' compensation claims; and make attempts to locate missing persons. Most detectives find it effective to specialize in one particular field of investigation. These specializations generally fall under five categories:

☞ *Legal investigators* generally work directly for law firms. They are charged with completing all research necessary to prepare a criminal defense. This may include gathering witnesses, interviewing police, serving legal documents, or reviewing evidence. Often they must testify in court.

☞ *Corporate investigators* are assigned cases that affect businesses inside or out. They may attempt to determine whether employees are abusing company policies, using illicit drugs at work, or engaging in industrial espionage. They also protect the company from being taken advantage of by their competitors.

☞ *Financial investigators* look for clues to fraudulent behavior in the financial records of companies. They are often engaged to investigate a company's assets before a corporate merger to ensure they are transparent.

☞ *Computer forensic investigators* are likely to benefit most from growth within the field thanks to the surge of computer-based crimes, such as identity theft, e-mail harassment, or illegal downloading. They focus on recovering and analyzing data from computers, often circumventing encryption or password protection in order to gather evidence.

☞ *Loss prevention agents* work for retail stores or hotels and work to prevent customers from stealing merchandise, or protect hotel guests from being victimized by thieves.

Your background can help you decide what specialization for which you would be most suited. If you have previous experience working in security, you may be interested in pursuing a career as a loss prevention agent. If you have a business degree, corporate investigation may be more appealing. Where you make your home also can help you choose what type of investigation you would most like to focus on. Most of states require that private investigators obtain licensing, yet each state has different criteria. Also, many detectives choose to carry a weapon for personal protection, or if they are working as bodyguards. It is compulsory to have a firearms permit in all states. However, once you have the appropriate authorizations, there is absolutely nothing stopping you from getting right to work. Investigators generally do work alone and have little need for a professional office; much of the labor will be done anywhere from corporate boardrooms to beaten-down rooming houses. And with the onset of increased concerns about security, growth in litigation, and the proliferation of identity theft, private investigation is a vocation that will only increase in demand over the next 10 years.

You Are Here

Set yourself on the path to becoming a private investigator.

Do you have ingenuity? It is best to think of an investigation as a vast connect-the-dots game. By sorting through a passel of small details, a good detective will be able to see the complete picture. Being able to process a large amount of seemingly divergent information is a must. It is also best to have the memory of an elephant; or, barring that, a detail-oriented personality and the foresight to take excellent notes. Many detectives are compelled to testify in court in order to help close the cases they have undertaken. If you cannot provide clear, concise, and believable testimony under oath, you will find your client base quickly drying up. On that note, it is also necessary to hone your interrogation skills. With good preparation and some assertiveness, it will be possible for you to get the answers you need from even a very reticent individual.

Are you adaptable? One of the most important qualities found in a private investigator is the ability to roll with the punches. Much of your training will take place on the job and it is likely that rather than undergo a long period of desk work to ready yourself, your supervisor could send you straight into the field—a trial by fire, indeed. As a greenhorn detective, you set out some afternoon to do what you think is a routine interview with a clerk at the local planning office and end up pursuing a lead into a seedy tavern, only to suddenly find yourself in a less than congenial environment at a less than savory hour. Can you think on your feet? Talk your way out of a bad situation? Have a fair amount of courage and the wherewithal to fake the rest? If you enjoy making the best out of every bad situation, private investigation may be just the work you have been seeking.

Do you enjoy your own company? If you are a person who enjoys a collaborative work environment, private investigation is not the career for you. Most private investigators work for themselves. It is a solitary pursuit spent following leads, conducting interviews, running computer searches, and making phone calls. Without the help of a support staff, it is up to you to not only provide satisfactory service to your clients, but also act as your own assistant, scheduler, marketer, advertising representative, and—if you keep an office—janitor. When you are not working on a case, you will be out drumming up more business for yourself. Your hours will be irregular and often long, centering on nights and weekends. But if you are inclined to work alone, at the very least you can take comfort in only having yourself and your own safety to worry about.

Organizing Your Expedition

Get everything in order as you prepare to become a private investigator.

Decide on a destination. Many detectives have backgrounds in law enforcement or criminal justice. In fact, because police officers generally retire rather young, it is common to find agencies staffed entirely by ex-law enforcement officers. Often detectives have previously served in the military. Many corporate investigators were once accountants or business administrators. Computer forensic investigators may have once worked in the field in information technologies. Although many do have bachelor's degrees, it is not necessary in order to become a private investigator. Most detectives draw on their prior life experiences to enhance their investigation techniques. They learn the trade by plying it, not in a classroom.

Scout the terrain. As noted in the introduction to this chapter, each state has differing requirements for those new to the private investigation field. Your first step is to contact your local state department of public safety, state division of licensing, or state police department to determine the requirements in your own state. You should also be aware that most private investigators that seek work in an agency will be subject to a criminal background check. Private investigators are essentially public safety officers who work without the benefits of a badge. Take the

Navigating the Terrain

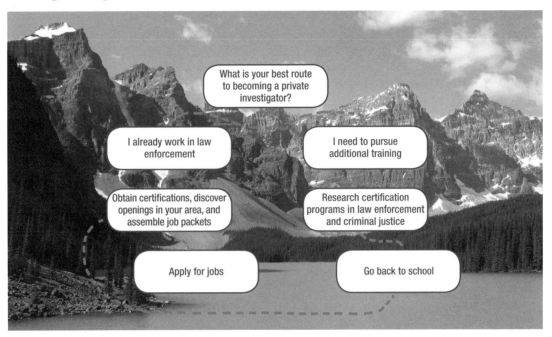

What is your best route to becoming a private investigator?

I already work in law enforcement

I need to pursue additional training

Obtain certifications, discover openings in your area, and assemble job packets

Research certification programs in law enforcement and criminal justice

Apply for jobs

Go back to school

time to familiarize yourself with the federal, state, and local legislation governing privacy laws in your region. Also, if you have no prior experience collecting evidence, you should look into enrolling in an appropriate course at a college that offers classes in police science—you do not want to be at fault for tainting evidence that would have otherwise led to a closed court case.

Find the path that's right for you. Ask yourself this question: Am I more comfortable working in an office environment or on the street? There are positions available that can fit into everyone's lifestyle and comfort zone. If sitting in your car for 10 hours with a camera and a bagged lunch does not appeal to you, corporate, legal, financial, and computer forensic investigators most often rely on computers to provide them the data they need to complete an investigation. But if you thrive on constant change and stimulation, it may be a better fit for you to perform physical surveillance, conduct interviews, or work undercover to obtain the information you are seeking. Be aware that you will face stiff competition from many

Notes from the Field
Alice Byrne
President and CEO, Alice Byrne Investigations, Inc.
Brooklyn, New York

What were you doing before you decided to become a private investigator?
I was a registered nurse working in St. Vincent's Hospital in Manhattan.

Why did you decide to pursue a career as a private investigator?
An opportunity suddenly presented itself to do something for El Al Israel Airlines and on the spur of the moment I said, "I'll do that!" I don't know why I did except that it sounded exciting. I worked under another person's license for three years and then got my own. I learned from the Israelis and retired NYPD detectives I hired. There are no better teachers.

What was involved in terms of education and training?
My training in psychiatric nursing actually helped me a great deal. I knew how to closely observe people and listen to not only the words they were saying, but what the thoughts behind those words might be. I could detect signs of nervousness or deception more easily, and understand certain behaviors as it fit into their personalities. As a nurse I had to write accurate, descriptive reports and this helped me in my investigative work. I developed quite a bit of confidence and the ability

qualified people. Detective is a title that appeals to not only ex–police officers seeking a second career, but to those who respond to its romantic allure. If you are able to convey your seriousness in pursuing private investigation to any prospective employers, you should be well on your way to fulfilling your own dream of cracking the case.

Landmarks

If you are in your twenties . . . Computer forensics is the fastest growing field within investigations, and those who are able to pursue that line of work are most likely to find a lasting career in private investigation. A *to deal with all kinds of situations as a nurse, and that all transferred over to starting my company and being here 39 years later.*

What are the keys to success and the qualities of a good private investigator?

I believe attention to detail is one of the major keys in being a good investigator. The ability to really listen and keep detailed, accurate records is also key. I believe a good investigator has to be very adaptable to all kinds of situations especially in working undercover or interviewing uncooperative witnesses. I also think showing empathy and respect for your clients is a very important characteristic of a good investigator. A good investigator has to be creative in thought and action.

What surprised you the most about your role as a private investigator?

What surprised me the most about my career has been how one opportunity led to another and then another. I went to a meeting of women business owners where they were demonstrating how to write a press release. I needed it for a missing child case. Three years later I was president of Women Business Owners of New York. That led me to on a whim invite the president of the United States to lunch at our annual meeting. President Reagan accepted and the next day our picture was on the front page of the New York Times. He then helped me with missing kids and the development of Child Find of America, Inc. As the honorary national chair, I am proud to say that organization has helped locate 2,800 missing kids all pro bono. Many opportunities have come my way and I am very grateful for them all.

computer science degree can be very helpful, but alternatively many colleges and universities now offer certification programs in forensics. It may be beneficial to check with your local colleges to find out whether they offer a program that would be suitable for you.

If you are in your thirties or forties . . . If you do not have prior experience in law enforcement that you can bring with you to the private sector, courses in criminal justice and police science can help a would-be detective become more attractive to potential employers. There you can begin to make contacts in the field of private investigation that, along with your newfound knowledge, can later lead to a position with an agency.

If you are in your fifties . . . Can you bring the experience you gained in your prior job to your new career as a private investigator? Many legal investigators began as lawyers or paralegals, financial investigators as accountants or bankers. Use the skills you already have to your advantage to help you land a position as a detective.

Essential Gear

Stay on the cutting edge of computers. Computers are the key to effective investigations. They allow investigators, with minimal effort, to obtain vast quantities of information, such as telephones numbers, previous addresses, motor vehicles registrations, prior arrest records or convictions, and photographs. Take all opportunities to familiarize yourself with every new database, operating system, piece of software, and method of fraud detection that is available to you. It can be the difference between slogging through a moldy filing cabinet for five hours, or finding exactly what you need with five minutes and a few keystrokes.

If you are over sixty . . . Bringing a wealth of life experience to your new role as a detective is an advantage. However, it would be unfair not to mention that private investigation can be physically demanding at times. Rather than look for positions as a loss prevention agent, which can involve the foot pursuit of a perpetrator, use your previous work experience to select a good match in a specialized, office-based field.

Further Resources

The **National Association of Legal Investigators (NALI)** is an internationally recognized organization for investigators specializing in litigation investigations. http://www.nalionline.org

ASIS International is the top organization for security professionals and features educational resources, administers three internationally accredited certification programs, and offers access to more than 22,000 security professionals from all over the world. http://www.asisonline.org

PI Magazine is the only recognized trade magazine for the investigative fields. Their comprehensive online presence of includes state-by-state listings of private investigator associations throughout the United States, information on upcoming conferences and seminars, and in-depth articles. http://www.pimagazine.com

Antiterrorism Consultant

Antiterrorism Consultant

Career Compasses

Guide yourself to a career as an antiterrorism consultant.

Relevant knowledge of the business systems that must be secured (30%)

Communication Skills to clearly relay security findings to the clientele (30%)

Organizational Skills to refine large quantities of information into a practical plan of action (20%)

Mathematical Skills to work with computers and other high-tech systems (20%)

Destination: Antiterrorism Consultant

Since the September 11 attacks on the World Trade Center and the Pentagon, the career profile of those working in the antiterrorism field has risen sharply. Indeed, the field of antiterrorism consulting has attracted such luminaries as Richard A. Clarke, who served as a top counterterrorism advisor in both Bill Clinton and George W. Bush's White Houses; Rudy Giuliani, former mayor of New York City; and John Ashcroft, the United States Attorney General under George W. Bush. Each of them has started his own antiterrorism consulting firm since departing his governmental position. However, many antiterrorism consultants had been at work long before that day in 2001.

Antiterrorism is different from counterterrorism, which is an offensive stance against terror attacks. The U.S. Department of Defense defines antiterrorism as "defensive measures used to reduce the vulnerability of individuals and property to terrorist acts." Antiterrorism consultants work with government agencies; nuclear and chemical plants; water treatment facilities; seaports, airports, or transportation hubs; banks and financial institutions; and other organizations that may be targeted by terrorists. It is the responsibility of the antiterrorism consultant to determine what threats or vulnerabilities affect an organization and what measures will secure it against an attack. These are referred to as "risk mitigation solutions." The central technique with which every antiterrorism consultant is familiar is the operations security assessment (OPSEC). Originally created for the use of the U.S. military, its concept is at the foundation of all antiterrorism work. The OPSEC assessment has five stages: (1) identification of critical information; (2) analysis of threats; (3) analysis of vulnerabilities; (4) assessment of risk; and (5) application of appropriate measures. These steps are the very same as those used by many antiterrorism consulting firms to assess their clientele.

Essential Gear

Firearms training. Most antiterrorism consultants work in office environments. However, if you wish to pursue work in the field offering security to at-risk individuals it will be necessary to carry a weapon. Learn to shoot and maintain a variety of firearms safely and properly. You may never need it to use it, but you may feel better that it is there.

To assess an organization for antiterrorist measures, the consultant must look at the following things: the general security of the organization, including mail screening, employee identification, and surveillance; the building in which the organization is located and how well it protects against chemical, biological, or explosive attacks; and the specific technical and information security of the organization. Business continuity planning is also taken into consideration. The consultant will then draw up a framework to help the organization seal any leaks in the organization. The organization can then decide whether to utilize their own staff to correct these issues, or they can make use of the consultant's resources. If an organization decides to work directly with the staff of the consulting firm, contractors working under the advisement of the consultant will begin coaching the organization's employees in shoring up the existing infrastructure. This may include installing new security technology, such as sensors that can detect airborne chemicals or explosives, biological recognition systems for employees, and video surveillance systems. They will also work with information security consultants to reinforce the data security of the organization. Similarly, many antiterrorism consultants apply this same knowledge to disaster management programs. Rather than preparing an organization for a terror threat, a consultant will plan for regularly threatened hurricanes, earthquakes, tornados, or other natural disasters.

Essential Gear

Laptop. You will want to carry and maintain your own computer for traveling to meet with clientele. This way, you are not tethered to an office, and will be able to run simulations, security checks, or install software for an organization without relying on their own infrastructure. In this day and age, it is impossible to work as a consultant unless you can travel with your "office."

Many antiterrorism consulting firms offer special security details, such as protective services for high-level corporate executives who may be the target of kidnapping. This can include travel security, handling ransom demands, and coordinating with local or federal law enforcement. In a related task, antiterrorism consulting firms routinely perform investigations or intelligence work. So as to not interfere with local or federal law enforcement, most of the investigative work done by consulting firms consists of background checks of employees and other contractors, as well as vendors and possible business partners. These investigations will not only uncover any criminal background or other suspicious behavior, but can also provide psychological profiling of a subject.

The background of most antiterrorism consultants consists most often of military service—especially special forces—or law enforcement. However, it is not unusual to find an antiterrorism specialist with an advanced college degree. In fact, many colleges and universities now offer studies in antiterrorism and security analysis. Additionally, many consulting firms require that their prospective employees pursue certification through their own training programs. And as enemies at home and abroad continue to threaten the safety of the United States, there will be continued employment growth for anyone talented enough to turn an organization into a fortress.

You Are Here

Set yourself on the path to becoming an antiterrorism consultant.

Are you a problem solver? Strong analytical skills are required of anyone interested in pursuing a career as an antiterrorism consultant. Because the nature of the work is to collect large quantities of information and distill it into a workable action plan, a successful antiterrorism consultant will have excellent problem-solving and organizational skills and be a creative thinker. If an aspect of a security plan is not operating as intended, it is the responsibility of the antiterrorism consultant to find a suitable solution. An antiterrorism consultant must have this resiliency to not become discouraged by any disappointments and instead work toward the future of the industry.

Do you stay current with new security techniques? In order to best serve your clientele, it is important to stay current with all industry requirements and technology. The best way to keep on top of recent developments is to subscribe not only to the trade magazines that offer information about the antiterrorism industry, but any periodicals that cover the technology that you will be using on a day-to-day basis: software, hardware, security tactics, and more. Plus, if you plan to focus your efforts on the security aspects of the field, it will be of great reassurance if you have the most up-to-date equipment necessary to protect both your client and yourself.

Do you want to work for yourself? The field of antiterrorism is very difficult to break into as an independent contractor. The most successful independent consultants have always started out with an extensive list of contacts, as well as years of practical experience, obtained from years spent working with a noteworthy firm. However, if you do not wish to align yourself with a preexisting antiterrorism consulting firm, it will be necessary to solicit your own business. Research the organizations in your area that would be in need of the type of service you plan to provide. This could be hospitals, chemical manufacturing plants, nuclear power stations, businesses within the financial service sector, and many others. Attempt to determine where some of their vulnerabilities lie. Then prepare a specific presentation that outlines how you could help to secure these organizations. If you are able to provide clients with a relatable, true-to-life scenario, it will be easier to convince them that there is a need for what you offer. When you are just starting out in the field, you may find that you need to undercut the competition in order to obtain work. Make sure you have a reserve of capital to fall back on until you can build up your clientele.

Organizing Your Expedition

Get everything in order as you prepare to become an antiterrorism consultant.

Decide on a destination. There are many facets of the antiterrorism field. Consultants generally work to bring all of these aspects together for their clientele. However, you can specialize in technology installation, computer information security, or obtain employment as a part of a private guard service that works with an antiterrorism consulting group. But whatever you choose, it is important to gain experience outside of the field while you investigate what interests you most. Seek an entry-level position working on a security detail, or with a corporate information technology department. Many who work in the antiterrorism sector have served in the military's special forces, especially those who aspired to a government position during their career. Choose a field closest to what you would eventually like to specialize in when employed in the antiterrorism sector. This will help to build your résumé and make you more appealing to potential employers at consulting firms.

Scout the terrain. The best way to seek out available positions in the antiterrorism field is to first begin by compiling a list of consulting firms in your area. Most of the largest firms are located in Washington, D.C., or New York City because of their close proximately government agencies, as well as possible terror targets. However, there may other possibilities all over the country. It may be that a local nuclear plant maintains a private security team. Often celebrities and notable individuals hire their own specialist to ensure that their safety is guaranteed. You may be able

Navigating the Terrain

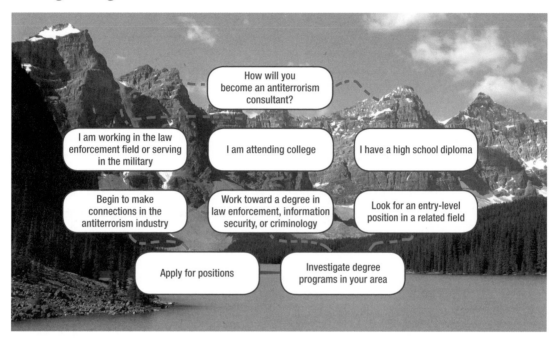

How will you become an antiterrorism consultant?

I am working in the law enforcement field or serving in the military

I am attending college

I have a high school diploma

Begin to make connections in the antiterrorism industry

Work toward a degree in law enforcement, information security, or criminology

Look for an entry-level position in a related field

Apply for positions

Investigate degree programs in your area

to gain employment with a company that designs and manufactures the technology used by antiterrorism consultants. If you live in an area that is frequently hit by hurricanes or tornados, you may want to look into a career specializing in disaster management and business continuity specifically. The antiterrorism field, despite what sounds like a specialized title, is actually a very wide-ranging area, and the tools that you acquire can be applied to many different industries.

Find the path that's right for you. Once you have some work experience and have selected a number of consulting firms that interest you, make appointments to speak with either a human resources or a public relations representative at each firm. Prepare a list of questions that you have about the antiterrorism industry, as well as an honest assessment of your own skills. The nature of a fact-finding mission like this is twofold: first, you will be able to get a clear idea of what an antiterrorism consulting firm is seeking in candidates for employment, and second, you will get valuable face time with a member of that firm who may then be able to help you find suitable employment once your training is complete.

Notes from the Field

Maren Leed
Senior fellow, Center for Strategic and International Studies
Washington, D.C.

What were you doing before you decided to become an antiterrorism consultant?

I have worked on antiterrorism issues in the context of various jobs. I was working in the defense field as an analyst, and was provided with the opportunity to work for a senior military officer. I chose to do this because I thought it would give me great exposure to national security issues at the highest levels. Part of my responsibilities in this position was to work on terrorism-related issues with various organizations within and outside the Department of Defense.

Why did you decide to pursue a career in defense?

I sort of fell into the defense field in my first job after college, and stayed with it because I found it interesting. I enjoyed working with military personnel, and have always been challenged by the wide range of public policy issues the defense establishment must address, from education (of military members and their children) to health care to warfare.

Some consulting firms work with their own private training facilities. You may want to research whether or not attending these programs will greatly enhance your prospects of finding employment down the road.

Landmarks

If you are in your twenties . . . If you have no previous work experience in the field of antiterrorism, it will be best to pursue a degree in law enforcement, information security, or criminology, especially if you know for certain that this is the career path for you. Research schools in your area that offer these majors. You can also consider a joining the military. This is an easy transition into the antiterrorism area and has the added bonus of granting you the money to attend college once you have completed your term of service.

What was involved in terms of education and training?

Much of it was on-the-job training, although I made a conscious effort to try to work on defense and terrorism issues in a variety of stakeholder organizations: Congress, think tanks, and within the Department of Defense. I also pursued a PhD in quantitative policy analysis in order to become more facile with quantitative methods, which have substantial weight in defense and terrorism policy decisions.

What are the keys to success?

The keys to success are an in-depth knowledge of some aspect of the issue, e.g. the international or national organizational structures and policy debates or the academic debate within a given discipline or disciplines. Relationships within the community of interest are critical. Important qualities include objectivity, cultural understanding, and open-mindedness.

What surprised you the most about your career?

How many policies are based on theories that have little or no factual or empirical underpinning.

If you are in your thirties or forties . . . If you have been working in a related field, make an appointment to speak with the human resources representative at a number of consulting firms. There, you can present your previous work experience and determine what will transfer to your new career. They will also give you information regarding any specialized training you will need to acquire before applying for positions.

If you are in your fifties . . . A computer hobbyist can easily transition into information technology, and then on to security. Turn the knowledge you gained at home into an entry-level placement with an information technology firm or department. Once you learn the ins and outs of corporate information technology support, you can begin to move into consulting for the information security sector.

If you are over sixty . . . Because many antiterrorism consultants work within an office environment, it is a good career for someone to pursue late in life. In fact, many ex-police officers and government agents pursue this work after retirement. Are there any previous experiences you can highlight as you look for employment?

Further Resources

The **International Association for Counterterrorism & Security Professionals (IACSP)** is a trade organization for professionals working in that field. Their Web site offers a center of informational and educational resources available not only to antiterrorism professionals, but also to anyone interested in understanding the field. http://www.iacsp.com

The **Operations Security Professional's Association** offers professional resources to anyone working in the OPSEC industry, including employment postings. http://www.opsecprofessionals.org

Planet Data covers news and topics of interest to those in the security sector. It includes information relevant to those in the global, aviation, corporate, information, homeland, and maritime security industries, as well as for those in law enforcement and intelligence. http://www.planetdata.net

The **Security Industry Association (SIA)** is an organization that offers news, education and training, as well as cutting-edge research on topics relating to the security industry. http://www.siaonline.org

The **United States Department of State's Bureau of Diplomatic Security** offers information about the specific threats to American's abroad. They also offer an antiterrorism assistance program—a service that provides antiterrorism training to law enforcement professionals as well as civilian security officers throughout the world. http://www.state.gov/m/ds/terrorism/c8583.htm

Forensic Science Technician

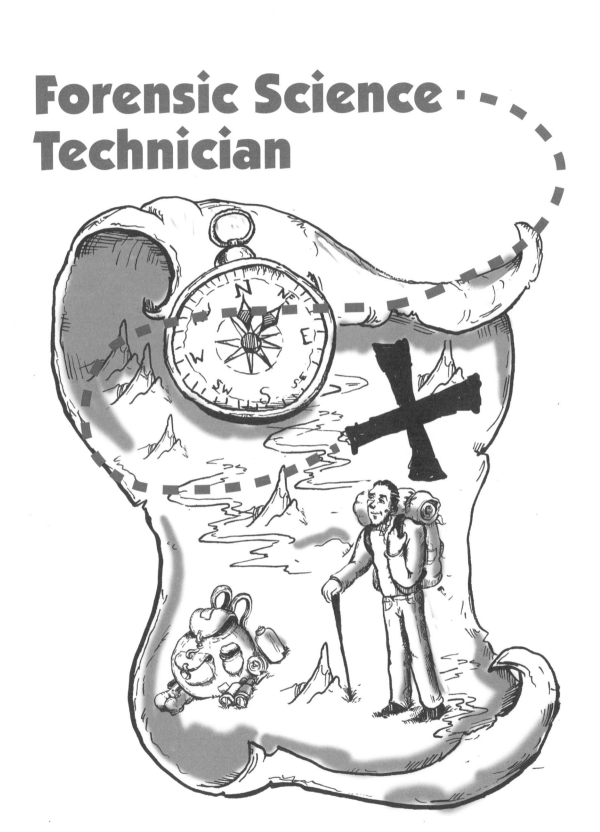

Forensic Science Technician

Career Compasses

Guide yourself to a career as a forensic science technician.

Relevant Knowledge to determine the appropriate scientific procedures and how to execute them (40%)

Organizational Skills to maintain the admissibility and integrity of numerous pieces of evidence (30%)

Communication Skills that enable the composition of detailed evidence reports and successful in-court testimony (20%)

Mathematical Skills for reading and understanding test results and measurements (10%)

Destination: Forensic Science Technician

When the program *CSI* debuted on television more than 10 years ago, it set off a flurry of interest in forensic science, and brought a previously low profile branch of law enforcement to the forefront of America's imagination. Despite its pop culture notoriety, for the right person the field of forensics can be a fascinating and satisfying career choice that combines the methodology of police work with the laboratory experience of the sciences.

A variety of forensic science technicians may work on any criminal investigation. It is specifically crime scene technicians who are called in by police immediately after an investigation is opened. They are the most methodical of the technicians. They are charged with collecting evidence from the crime scene without compromising or damaging what they find. The medical examiner/coroner inspects the victim of the accident or violent crime. The victim's clothing is searched for foreign fibers, scrapings are taken underneath the fingernails, and the hands are bagged. Any wounds are inspected and photographed, as are the placement of the victim and the surrounding area. The coroner also inspects the crime scene for any other evidence, such as bullet casings and any weapons, as well as evidence that can be difficult to spot, like fingerprints, hair, fibers, tissue, bodily fluids, or anything else that could harbor DNA evidence. They then safeguard the evidence against contamination and transport it to the crime lab.

Essential Gear

Learn the legalities. Knowing the ins and outs of the American legal system can greatly improve your appeal to potential employers. In fact, those who wish to pursue the field of forensic science often not only study science, but also pad their class schedule with plenty of courses in law, law enforcement, and criminal justice. It is a strategy that prospective employers will appreciate—they will feel more secure knowing that their newly hired forensic science technician knows exactly what evidence is admissible in court and how to keep it safeguarded.

Once this evidence arrives at the crime lab, the type of evidence collected determines what forensic science technicians will begin working to process it. If there are fingerprints available, for instance, a fingerprint identification technician will be called. Some forensic science technicians work in ballistics, examining bullet casings, gunshot residue, and bullet paths to determine how shootings occurred and whether a specific weapon was used to commit the crime. Others take photos, both at the scene and during the autopsy process. Still others ensure that the evidence is preserved and stored correctly until trial. In large metropolitan areas this breakdown is much more common. In less populated communities, only a small number of technicians may be employed, and all of them are trained to do a complete crime scene work-up.

All forensic science technicians move toward one common goal: interpret evidence collected at crime scenes to help the state either build a case against a suspect or identify the perpetrator so that they may be pursued by law enforcement. During this process, technicians work with a number of people—detectives, medical examiners/coroners, pathologists, and fire investigators are just a few of the possibilities. Using the tools available in the crime lab, technicians conduct a wide variety of tests. Some of the most common are analyzing biological matter to determine whether DNA is found and able to matched to a suspect; conducting toxicology reports on the victim; testing physical evidence like liquid, soil, hair, fiber, and possible weapons found at the crime scene to match them to their source; and reconstructing of crime scenes to develop a picture of the relationships among all of the available evidence. If more detailed reports are needed, a forensic science technician will call in an expert on a subject like ballistics, fingerprinting, handwriting, chemicals, or metallurgy to interpret questionable findings.

Essential Gear

Natural curiosity. "If at first you don't succeed, try and try again" could be the unofficial credo of a forensic science technician. When an initial theory does not prove correct, it is always tempting to throw our hands up in defeat. However, forensic science technicians are required to try and try again until a coherent picture of what took place during a crime begins to coalesce from all of the evidence provided. In this situation, a technician will instead try to look at the evidence in an entirely new way—a task made much easier when the technician is adept at thinking past the obvious to achieve a result.

When not devoted entirely to a particular case, the forensic science technician is busy maintaining laboratory equipment, including the preparation of solutions needed for laboratory testing. Forensic science technicians are also responsible for testifying in a court of law to the accuracy of their findings. In preparation, they maintain records and reports of their examinations, as well as a detailed log of how they came to their conclusions.

Nearly all aspiring forensic science technicians must hold at least a bachelor's degree in a science-related field if they hope to pursue a position. It is possible to receive a bachelor's degree in forensic science specifically; however, many technicians opt for a chemistry, biology, or natural science degree with additional classes in law enforcement, criminal justice, and law. Most of the programs in forensic science accredited by the

American Academy of Forensic Science take five years to complete. Also, there are further agency certifications that can be obtained to increase a technician's knowledge and employability. It is more difficult, but not impossible, to find a position in forensic science technology that will accept an associate's degree. Once employed, forensic science technicians often complete training programs under the advisement of a senior technician. Because forensic science technicians are generally employed by the state or federal government, and are considered a branch of law enforcement, those with a criminal record or anyone who cannot pass a drug screening will not be considered for employment, no matter how minor the youthful transgression may have been. Those who do find work in this fascinating field can look forward to a competitive salary and rapid growth in employment opportunities as new technologies and scientific advances begin to allow the world to fight and prevent crime in ways never before imagined.

You Are Here

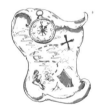

Set yourself on the path to becoming a forensic science technician.

Do you have an interest in the sciences? Despite what is shown on television, the role of a forensic science technician is above all that of a scientist: most of the work is laboratory-based. Those who find the most success in this field are those who counted math and sciences among their favorite subjects during high school. Those who hold a bachelor's degree in chemistry, biology, life sciences, or forensic science and have a solid background in laboratory work will be highly sought after by employers. It is difficult but not impossible to transition to forensic science from another field. Any aspiring forensic science technician will need to pursue at least an associate's degree in the sciences, no matter what prior education was received. Because of the nature of the work, a forensic science technician will be exposed to the aftermath of violent crimes such as homicide and rape, as well as automobile accidents and suicide. Forensic science technicians often are present while the medical examiner performs autopsies. One needs to be able to think of such grisly scenes as opportunities to explore the biological evidence and to avoid becoming emotionally affected by what one sees in the laboratory or morgue.

Are you meticulous, methodical, and patient? The sheer quantity of evidence a forensic science technician must sort through while conducting an investigation can be staggering. Imagine searching a bedroom carpet in its entirety to locate a shred of fiber; taking that shred to the laboratory; painstakingly examining it under a microscope to determine its make-up; comparing it to all of the textiles owned by a victim; and, barring a match, hoping to find out who manufactured it, where it is sold, and how it could have possibly made its way into the crime scene. If this sounds like a painstaking and lengthy process to you, know that this type of investigative work is very common in the field of forensic science. A person without the ability to stay the course in the face of such methodical and meticulous investigative work will be an unsuccessful technician.

Do you have excellent communication skills? Forensic science technicians are often called to testify in court as expert witnesses to explain the veracity of their findings and how these results impact the suspect in a crime. Because their laboratory tests can be complex and difficult to explain to a layperson, a technician must be able to translate everything from the correct usage of scientific instruments to an analysis of a toxicology report so that the lawyers, judge, and jury can understand. As a witness, a technician is compelled to tell the truth impartially, even if it will hurt the state's prosecution. While in the probationary period of their employment, or in preparation for an upcoming case, forensic science technicians will often reevaluate evidence and rehearse their testimony to make sure it is perfect before taking the stand.

Organizing Your Expedition

Get everything in order as you prepare to become a forensic science technician.

Decide on a destination. Those who consider themselves science or math-minded individuals who thrive when working under the constraints of a laboratory setting would find a satisfying career in forensic science. The job prospects are best for forensic science technicians who have at least a bachelor's degree. Approximately 30 colleges in the United States offer degree programs in forensic science specifically and 25 others offer a degree course in life sciences with a concentration in

Navigating the Terrain

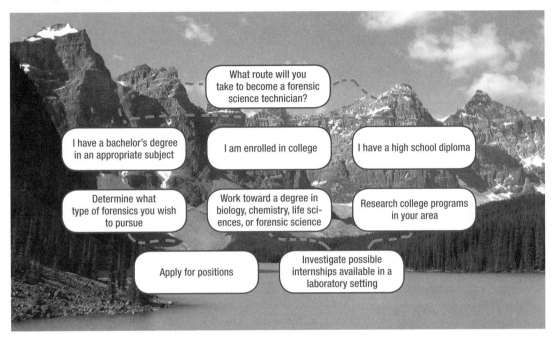

What route will you take to become a forensic science technician?

I have a bachelor's degree in an appropriate subject

I am enrolled in college

I have a high school diploma

Determine what type of forensics you wish to pursue

Work toward a degree in biology, chemistry, life sciences, or forensic science

Research college programs in your area

Apply for positions

Investigate possible internships available in a laboratory setting

forensics; however, almost any course of science can be adapted for the pursuit of forensic science. It is possible to enroll in a technical school's two-year general science program in order to better transition to a bachelor's degree program. Decide what path would work best for you. Will you require student loans to complete your education? If so, now is the time to choose the program you are most interested in and setting up financing to cover tuition, books, and laboratory costs, as well as housing if relocation is necessary.

Scout the terrain. While pursuing a degree, begin to look into either laboratory-based internships available through your school, or take a part-time position working in a laboratory environment. Some schools offer cooperative-education programs that will place you with a local laboratory that, if satisfied with your level of ability, will offer employment after graduation. When applying for positions after completing your degree, demonstrable experience in all varieties of scientific equipment, including computers, will be an asset to any employer. If you do

Notes from the Field
Jack Westwood
Owner, Chippewa Investigations
Laveen, Arizona

What were you doing before you decided to become a forensics specialist?

I have always been in law enforcement, beginning when I was 20 years old. I just moved up the chain from a street cop to detective, explosives expert, firearms expert, and then to full-blown forensics.

Why did you decide to pursue a career in forensics?

I decided about halfway through my police career that I wanted to do more hands-on investigative work, getting in the middle of the evidence.

What was involved in terms of education and training?

I have a bachelor's degree in criminology, a master's degree in criminal justice, and a Ph.D. in criminology/forensics.

not have this on your résumé, look for positions that offer on-the-job training. There is always a learning curve with any new career; however, the more preparation you do during your years in college can ease the transition considerably.

Find the path that's right for you. There are many places an aspiring forensic science technician can pursue employment. Most are employed by the federal, state, and local government in laboratories that work exclusively for law enforcement agencies. Most forensic science technicians begin as trainees. In that role, you will be exposed to police officers, medical examiners, attorneys, and more. Your interactions with these colleagues as well as those you work with in the laboratory can help to influence your future career path. If you find yourself fascinated by the autopsy process, you may wish to pursue further education in pathology. If you enjoy working with detectives on criminal investigation, you should explore a placement with the crime scene investigation team. Forensic science technicians can often dovetail their career with their interests. Another option for employment as a forensic science technician is with hospitals, universities, or with specialized forensics laboratories.

What are the keys to success and the qualities of a good forensics specialist?

Never consider any piece of evidence worthless until you have exhausted every means of testing to see if it contains anything useable. Always recheck your work to make sure that you never missed anything and that you covered all the bases.

What surprised you the most about your role as a forensics specialist?

I do not think I have ever been surprised in my 50 years in this business. I have always had a second sense about everything and I have always followed my instincts in every case I have every worked, which if I had kept count would be in the thousands by now, and I have enjoyed every minute.

One new possibility for specialized forensic science employment lies with the Federal Emergency Management Association (FEMA). In the event of a national emergency or large-scale criminal investigation, teams from the Disaster Mortuary Operations Response Team (DMORT) are sent to assist local forensic department with identifying victims.

Landmarks

If you are in your twenties . . . Begin by researching degree programs that offer forensic science as a major. Pursuing your bachelor's degree in this specific subject will make it much easier to obtain employment after graduation. If you are currently enrolled in college, determine whether your current major is complimentary to the field of forensic science. If not, consider switching to a course of science.

If you are in your thirties or forties . . . If you have a college degree in biology, chemistry, or life sciences, and experience in a laboratory setting, you are well-prepared for a career as a forensic science technician. If you do not any previous experience, you could explore a laboratory internship or a two-year program at a technical school that can help bring you up to speed on the new technologies and general scientific advances that have impacted the forensic sciences.

If you are in your fifties . . . Have you previously held positions in law enforcement, the medical industry, or law? If so, your work experience in those settings may allow for you to transfer into the field of forensic sciences. It will be necessary to take a few classes in laboratory procedures, but by utilizing your professional contacts, a position as a forensic science technician will not be out of reach.

If you are over sixty . . . When a degree is required for employment, changing careers late in life is always a challenge. If you do not wish to attend a training program or obtain a four-year degree, instead carefully review your job experience. What previous positions fit with the criteria for employment as a forensic science technician? Tailor your résumé to highlight these jobs then pursue available positions that offer on-the-job training.

Further Resources

The **American Academy of Forensic Sciences** is an international multidisciplinary professional organization committed to the promotion of education and the elevation of accuracy, precision, and specificity in the forensic sciences and its applications to the law. The Web site offers a wealth of information for those interested in pursuing a career in a field of forensic sciences. http://www.aafs.org

Carpenter's Forensic Science Resources is a comprehensive Web site that offers detailed descriptions of the various disciplines found in the forensic sciences including crime scene investigation and DNA analysis, and links to organizations and societies for forensic science professionals. http://www.tncrimlaw.com/forensic

The **United States Department of Energy** details the various genome projects being conducted by their Office of Science, including the human genome project. The Web site also offers examples and applications of this information in the field of DNA forensics. http://genomics.energy.gov

Firefighter

Firefighter

Career Compasses

Guide yourself to a career as a firefighter.

Relevant Knowledge to access the emergency situation to determine the best way to combat fire or handle other emergency situations (30%)

Ability to Manage Stress when in dangerous and life-threatening situations (30%)

Organizational Skills to manage equipment in a team-based situation (20%)

Communication Skills to effectively work with other firefighters (20%)

Destination: Firefighter

The firefighter is arguably one of the most beloved figures in any community. Nevertheless, it is also one of the more dangerous and uncertain career paths one could embark on. Not only is the risk of bodily harm very high, but it can be quite difficult to find employment. It is a career that one must demonstratively want, badly. Many aspiring firefighters wait years, often while working on a volunteer basis or in a related field like emergency medical services, to find a full-time position with a fire department.

Many municipalities are converting their volunteer fire companies to paid positions, so the field is expected to see some growth. It is likely that the demand for positions will exceed the number of those that are created. This is not only because many people are naturally drawn to the challenges of the field; firefighting is also one of the few careers that requires no post-high school education. Each fire department instead offers its own training program to recruits. However, it is not unusual these days to find firefighters with a college education.

A firefighter on duty can expect a number of scenarios. Most commonly, he or she spends shift hours at the station house maintaining equipment. When facing a fire, all firefighters have is this collection of tools. It is of the utmost importance that they are in proper working order at all times. An equipment failure can lead to injury or death. During an emergency call, firefighters begin by assessing the situation. What does the call require? Is it a fire, automobile accident, or some other issue? This information will come into the station

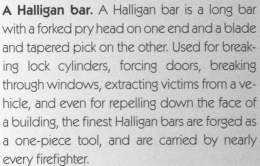

Essential Gear

A Halligan bar. A Halligan bar is a long bar with a forked pry head on one end and a blade and tapered pick on the other. Used for breaking lock cylinders, forcing doors, breaking through windows, extracting victims from a vehicle, and even for repelling down the face of a building, the finest Halligan bars are forged as a one-piece tool, and are carried by nearly every firefighter.

through an emergency dispatcher. Once the firefighters reach the scene, they quickly unload whatever equipment is needed and take the position dictated by their superior officer. Some firefighters will man the hoses, others will break through doors or walls to gain entrance to a structure and fight the fire from within, and still others will comb through a building in search of anyone left inside. This last role of rescuer is often the most dangerous and athletic assignment a firefighter can receive. If he or she encounters a person who cannot move due to smoke inhalation or other injury, the firefighter must remove the person from the building by carrying them out. As the emergency situation changes as the fire is brought under control, the role each firefighter plays may also change. In cases of extreme disasters, such as September 11, firefighters may stay at a site for days searching for survivors and providing medical treatment.

There are a few different settings in which a prospective firefighter can hope to find work. The most common is a city fire department. Other firefighters find placements with nuclear facilities, chemical plants, or with industries required to maintain a private fire department. Another exciting specialization is forest fires. This type of firefighter is often called a "smoke jumper." This position involves parachuting into areas where forest fires and wildfires are reported and attempting to quell them by creating new fires, clearing brush, cutting down trees, and digging trenches. Because the areas where these types of fires thrive are very remote and the wind can change direction in moments, these firefighters are at a greater risk for injury. The majority of smoke jumpers are centered in the western half of the United States, where wildfires are commonplace. Another option is to become a fire inspector or fire investigator. Inspectors are a part of the fire prevention division and verify that buildings are compliant with fire codes, while investigators are similar to police detectives in that they determine the causes of fires by collecting evidence.

Essential Gear

Be kind to animals. Dogs, particularly the Dalmatian breed, have long been a part of firefighting lore. Originally used to help calm the horses that pulled the fire rigs before the advent of cars, they are companions and mascots in many fire stations. Many fire companies have begun utilizing arson dogs. These specially trained canines use their sense of smell to isolate the cause of a fire. The management of these dogs could become a new source of employment in the industry. On a lighter note, firefighters also conduct a fair amount of animal rescues. It turns out the image of a kindly firefighter gently removing a cat from a tree is not too far from the truth!

Though the salary for most firefighters is fairly modest, much like police officers, they are compensated with a generous benefits and pension package. Firefighters can improve their pay by pursuing promotions—all gained through examination. These advanced titles include engineer, lieutenant, captain, battalion chief, assistant chief, deputy chief, and chief. With each promotion, a firefighter can expect a higher salary, as well as much more responsibility for directing the actions of the men and women underneath them and the actions of the department as a whole. Remember, only the highest-scoring hopefuls will receive not only their first shot as a firefighter, but a chance at these rankings. However, if an aspiring firefighter does manage to be selected for one of these coveted positions, he or she can look forward to a steady career as a figurehead of the community.

You Are Here

Set yourself on the path to becoming a firefighter.

Would you consider yourself fearless? As a firefighter, you will be running into burning buildings, collapsing structures, and performing high-stakes rescue efforts. You will be exposed to smoke, chemicals, poisonous gases, and sometimes even radioactive materials. The risk of grave injury or death is always looming large. Yet when an alarm sounds, a firefighter cannot hesitate for one moment. Those firefighters who specialize in forest work are even more at risk. Not only do they often parachute into remote areas, but they are immediately in danger and far from help should the wind shift or if one of the crew is injured. Most firefighters claim that their desire to help those in need—and good old adrenaline—overrides any panic they may feel. Be sure that concern for your family and for yourself will not inhibit you from doing the job.

Essential Gear

Stay strong. Firefighting is a very physical career. The protective gear is heavy and bulky; pressurized water hoses are difficult to hold; doors are broken down; and firefighters must scale buildings using ladders, stairs, and sometimes ropes. Firefighters are responsible for getting victims out of emergency situations as quickly as possible without further risking themselves or the injured. If that means carrying them, then that is what they are required to do. Firefighters regularly work out with weights and continually seek to improve their cardiovascular health. All aspiring firefighters should plan to keep their gym membership up to date!

Do you prefer an irregular schedule? The wife of a firefighter once joked that she planned to print up a T-shirt to read "He's at the station" to deflect the most common question asked at family and community functions. But it is absolutely the case that firefighters work very irregular hours and, while on duty, live at station house. Most firefighters can expect a shift of 24 hours on, 48 hours off. Some stations order a day shift of 10 hours for three to four days, followed by a night shift of 14 hours for three to four nights, followed by a few days off. Firefighters are often required to work a share of holidays and pull overtime during emergency situations. The accommodations at the station house are similar to that of a dormitory: bunk beds, communal kitchens, and bathrooms. Many firefighters enjoy the camaraderie cultivated in this type of situation—shopping, cooking, cleaning, maintenance—all done as a group. It does help to solidify the team mentality, so that when summoned for an emergency everyone is more in tune with one another and able to work toward a common goal.

Are you willing to dedicate off-hours to additional training? Because the schedule is demanding, firefighters cherish what free time they do have. However, the science of firefighting is constantly evolving. It is necessary to stay on top of the newest technologies, methods, and safety equipment. Fire stations often require their employees to attend off-site classes to learn about these new developments. Firefighters are also certified emergency medical technicians, and are sometimes required to be licensed paramedics. These certifications are up for renewal on a regular basis. If a firefighter wishes to prepare for a promotion exam, he or she must begin to acquire proficiency in building construction, writing, public speaking, accounting, and public relations. The higher the position reached, the more responsibility falls to firefighters to involve themselves in community relations.

Navigating the Terrain

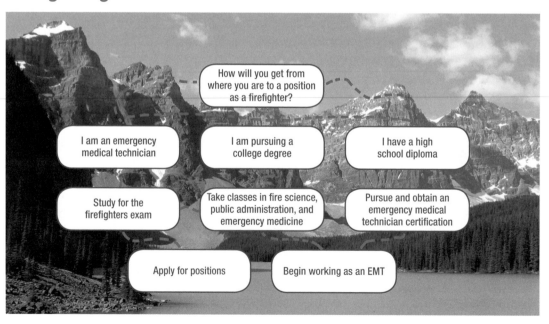

Organizing Your Expedition

Get everything in order as you prepare to become a firefighter.

Decide on a destination. The first step to a career in firefighting is determining the location of the highest number of available positions. Cities have especially large fire departments, as there is a risk of a fire or other emergency affecting a number of buildings. In the past, many rural fire companies were volunteer-only; this is still the case in a few areas of the country. However, most fire departments are switching to paid positions as the population increases throughout the country. If you are serious about becoming a firefighter, it may be necessary to relocate. Research the fire departments within your current locale, slowly expanding your search outward until you reach a location that seems to have a high number of available positions or a large number of fire companies.

Scout the terrain. Most fire departments will advertise when they are seeking applicants. Check local newspapers and municipal Web sites regularly. In these advertisements, departments will indicate the date and time that the firefighters exam will be administered. Be sure to make an appointment, if necessary, and arrive early! If there are more applicants than can be accommodated, the department will likely turn away any latecomers. Once the exam is complete, an applicant will be required to take a physical fitness test, medical examination, and a drug screening. Often, only those with the highest scores on the exam will be invited for further assessment.

Find the path that's right for you. Once an applicant is offered a position and accepts it, the real test begins. Fire companies require entry-level recruits to complete a number of education sessions at their own training facility, where firefighting techniques, prevention, hazardous material control, building codes, and emergency medical procedures are taught both in classroom and hands-on settings. The educational program also includes classes in the proper use and maintenance of all of the firefighting and rescue equipment, such as axes, extinguishers and hoses, and ladders. Many firefighters also choose to attend training programs with

Notes from the Field
James Schneider
Fireman first grade, FDNY
New York, New York

Why did you decide to pursue a career as a firefighter?

My father and uncles were volunteer firemen in Suffolk County, New York, while I was growing up. I worked as a volunteer fireman, and enjoyed it, so it was an obvious career choice.

What was involved in terms of education and training?

In fire academy, I was taught basic knowledge in firefighting, calisthenics, and hands-on training in different evolutions. Also, much of the classroom time encompassed both fire and medical instruction.

What are the keys to success and the qualities of a good firefighter?

This can be answered in many ways. Having the knowledge of your job and to never stop learning more in this ever-changing world can help, both as a fireman and as an officer, should you decide to take the steps. But you

the U.S. National Fire Academy that focus on specialized topics such as disaster preparedness. The completion of these additional programs can lead to higher pay and promotions within a department.

Landmarks

If you are in your twenties . . . Because firefighters must also be emergency medical technicians, the best step is to obtain your certification. It takes time to find work as a firefighter, and many choose to work as EMTs while they pursue available openings. Since EMTs also respond to emergency situations, it is also an excellent way to get to know the firefighters in your community's department. They can give you the heads-up when they are seeking individuals to fill positions.

If you are in your thirties or forties . . . Before you pursue a career as a firefighter, it may be worthwhile to take some classes in fire science and emergency medicine, as well as become a certified emergency medical *really need the zeal, commitment, and dedication to do a job you may not come back from alive—this is what makes anyone a good fireman.*

What surprised you the most about your role as a firefighter?

Growing up around it and listening to the discussions my dad and other relatives would have, I knew the good and bad of the service of a fire-fighter. So I was not really surprised at what my job would encompass. The fire service has always taken on many challenges—both before and after 9/11.

However, I am dismayed by the general public, who seem to think we do nothing all day. Places are laying off firefighters and other emergency service workers at a time when they are still needed most. I hear how "nice it must be to get paid to sleep," yet these same people admit they could not do their nine to five jobs for 24 hours without getting any sleep. People are very misinformed about firefighting, but many unions still do nothing to counter these facts. Even so, given the chance to re-live my life, I would not change my choice of career.

technician. Most firefighters begin working in their twenties and acquire this knowledge as they go. When beginning this type of career later in life, you will want to have a leg up on the competition. With this education, you can begin taking the examinations for promotion as soon as your probationary period is finished.

If you are in your fifties . . . Do you have prior experience in construction or law enforcement? If so, it may be of interest to become a fire inspector or investigator. Because most municipalities are now combining their fire departments with other community services, you may not even need to train as a firefighter first. Instead, it may be possible to take classes in fire and building code or fire investigation, depending on which you are most qualified for, and then pursue open positions.

If you are over sixty . . . Do you have experience working with the public and good communication skills? A career as an emergency dispatcher may be close enough to the front lines of firefighting to satisfy a thirst for adventure. Firefighters rely heavily on their dispatchers. Good dispatchers get the trucks quickly and safely to the scene of an emergency, and they can also help to prevent injuries to the firefighters by thoroughly preparing them for what to expect at a scene.

Further Resources

Firefighting.org is a not-for-profit Web site offering classifieds, forums, news, and other information for working and aspiring firefighters. http://www.firefighting.org

The **International Association of Firefighters** represents nearly 300,000 professional fire and emergency medical service workers and is the primary advocate for the implementation of new equipment and training. http://www.iaff.org

The **National Fire Academy** provides information about professional qualifications and a list of colleges and universities offering two- or four-year degree programs in fire science or fire prevention. http://www.usfa.dhs.gov/nfa/index.htm

Emergency Medical Technician (EMT)/ Paramedic

Emergency Medical Technician (EMT)/Paramedic

Career Compasses

Guide yourself to a career as an emergency medical technician (EMT) or paramedic.

Relevant Knowledge of injuries often incurred in emergency situations and how to stabilize each one effectively (40%)

Ability to Manage Stress to make life-or-death decisions quickly and with assurance (30%)

Communications Skills to be able to make yourself understood to the people you are treating, as well as your partner, the firefighters working in tandem with you, and your radio dispatcher (20%)

Organizational Skills to maintain and service the medical equipment located in your ambulance and to determine the best route to the scene of an emergency (10%)

Destination: Emergency Medical Technician/Paramedic

Working in the emergency medical services (EMS) sector can be characterized as thrilling, exhilarating, and even action-packed. When an ambulance's sirens and flashing lights are engaged, heading to an emergency call could never be considered boring. However, the responsibilities within the EMS field are very serious. A single snap decision could mean the difference between life and death for someone awaiting treatment. Seconds truly matter and anything from a wrong turn while trying to reach a scene to an incorrect diagnosis can escalate the severity of an injury. Choosing a career in the emergency medical services is not a decision to be taken lightly. In doing so, you become the caretaker of someone who may be frightened, in pain, and completely reliant on you to get to safety and into the hands of medical professionals. It is a stressful and demanding career, but for those who find in it their calling, there is nothing more satisfying than spending each day helping to save lives.

Essential Gear

Flexibility. Not the kind of flexibility that comes from lots of yoga. What a successful EMT or paramedic requires is lots of scheduling flexibility. Emergencies are not on a timetable, and covering 24 hours of necessary shifts require most EMTs and paramedics to work irregular hours. Also, at the tail end of an eight-hour day, you may just find yourself on the job for hours more because of a fire or accident. It is your duty to remain at the scene until those in your care have received treatment, or you have transported them to the appropriate facility.

Within the emergency medical services, the National Registry of Emergency Medical Technicians (NREMT) recognizes five levels of certification. Each state requires a foundational certification in order to work as an EMT/paramedic. Once you are employed in the field, you must recertify every two years. The entry-level certifications consist of first responder and EMT-basic. Those trained at these levels have a proficiency that will allow them to provide basic care on scene and transport patients to the hospital safely and quickly. A certification at the basic level will also allow the EMT to not only assess the patient's condition, but to also manage respiratory, cardiac, and trauma emergencies. An EMT-intermediate (in which there are two levels, 1985 and 1999) has a more advanced certification; however, the complexity of care they are allowed to provide varies greatly from state-to-state. The highest level of certification is paramedic. Paramedics are able to offer the most extensive on-scene care by administering drugs orally and intravenously, interpreting electrocardiograms, and performing endotracheal intubations. The extent of care does vary from state-to-state. Taken together, all of these certification levels make up the emergency medical service sector.

Various placements within the emergency medical services include government third service agencies, fire departments, hospital-based ambulance services, private companies, industrial and special operations settings, and the military. Out of the 201,000 reported EMTs and paramedics working in 2006, approximately four out of 10 were employed by private ambulance companies. Three out of 10 worked for fire departments, public ambulance services, and emergency medical services, among other local government positions, and two out of 10 were staff members within a medical facility or hospital. Most full-time career EMTs and paramedics work in metropolitan areas; in rural areas all-volunteer ambulance corps are more common. Many paramedics go on to careers as ambulance dispatchers or firefighters. Often they attend advanced schooling while working as paramedics and train to become nurses, nurse practitioners, or physician assistants, among other health care professions.

Essential Gear

Hit the gym. EMT and paramedic positions are known for their physicality. You will be lifting people onto gurneys and into ambulances, often encountering many sets of stairs along the way. In fact, one of the most common injuries reported by EMTs and paramedics is back strain and injury. If you take steps to strengthen your body while still training for your certification, you will be able to stave off many of the common workplace aches and pains.

The emergency medical services industry is expected to have a much higher rate of growth than other industries. Within 10 years, it is estimated that 31,000 new jobs for EMTs and paramedics will be created as full-time employees replace volunteers. Because the baby boom generation—currently the largest percentage of the population in the United States—continues to age, the need for trained EMTs and paramedics will only increase.

It is impossible to predict when an EMT/paramedic will get a call, but when dispatched by a 911 operator, it is necessary to jump into action. An EMT/paramedic and his or her partner will immediately race to the scene—be it a fire, car accident, shooting, home-based injury, woman in labor, or other emergency—and coordinate with the police officers and firefighters who have arrived. There they assess the condition of the patient. This includes requesting any medical information from the injured person, including drug allergies and preexisting conditions. Making sure to follow medical guidelines, as well as staying within the boundaries of a particular emergency medical services certification level, the EMT/paramedic treats the injuries of the patient, or begins the process of transporting the patient to a medical facility. Often, certified paramedics will treat the patient at the site of the emergency call, or at the patient's home, and determine whether further medical care is required.

Transporting a patient can be physically taxing. If an injury is reported to involve the neck or back, the patient must be strapped to a backboard to immobilize the affected area before being placed into the ambulance. One member of the EMS team will remain in the back of the ambulance to monitor the patient while the other drives. Once at the medical facility, it is the responsibility of the EMT/paramedic to check the patient in and provide any necessary medical information regarding the patient's condition to the physicians and nurses. After the call is complete, the team will replace and restock any ambulatory supplies and decontaminate the ambulance before answering any other emergency calls.

EMTs/paramedics must work in all weather, indoors and out. Their hours are often unusual and shifts long. Many EMTs/paramedics work at least 50 hours a week, if not more. They can be exposed to infectious diseases, or caught in dangerous situations if attending the scene of a shooting or transporting a patient who becomes agitated. Yet despite these negatives, many who choose the career of an EMT/paramedic report positive levels of job satisfaction. If you are lucky enough to be placed in an EMS sector with a commitment to providing training incentives and motivation for EMTs and paramedics, the job satisfaction rate is even higher.

You Are Here

Set yourself on the path to becoming an EMT or paramedic.

Do you have excellent patience, composure, and communication skills? A large component of an effective EMT or paramedic is an ability to communicate with people who are injured. Patients could become alarmed if they are disoriented and do not understand that you are there to help them. It is understandable to want to move quickly in emergency situations, but one must be mindful not to speak abruptly to patients, or in a way that will make them feel as if you do not care about their injuries. It can take incredible discipline to remain a calm and soothing presence when time is of the utmost importance, but if patients sense that you have little sympathy, or if you express irritation, it could cause a borderline situation to become explosive. To limit the possibility of this, you must always be able to clearly state who you are and what you are doing to each patient, each step of the way.

Do you have a desire to help people? Many EMTs and paramedics say that a desire to help their community drove them to consider a career in the emergency medical service. That will be the basis of your work in the emergency medical service field. Each call you receive has at its base one truism: the person who summoned you has been hurt and needs medical assistance. A good EMT or paramedic will be able to provide that, no matter what, because of their empathy and their desire to be of assistance to their fellow citizens.

Do you possess good leadership skills and a sense of personal integrity? Most EMTs and paramedics work in teams of two. When you and your partner reach the site of an emergency, it is up to both of you to determine which patient each will treat (in the case of multiple patients), or who will handle what aspect of the patient's care. There is little time for arguing the pros and cons. If you have a good sense of your team's particular strengths and weaknesses as well as excellent leadership skills, it will work to your advantage to delegate the responsibilities to your team. Also, it is important that you are comfortable leading by example. If your partner is not reliable, then your life-saving ability is greatly diminished. If you see your partner acting inappropriately on the job, you must have the self-confidence and personal integrity not to allow that behavior to continue—especially when it could seriously impact the care a patient receives from your team.

Organizing Your Expedition

Get everything in order as you prepare to become an EMT or paramedic.

Decide on a destination. Most EMTs and paramedics seek work with their local fire or police departments. These positions often have the highest salaries, but irregular schedules. Those who require a more stable work schedule because of family obligations often seek employment with private ambulance companies. There you will be charged with providing

Navigating the Terrain

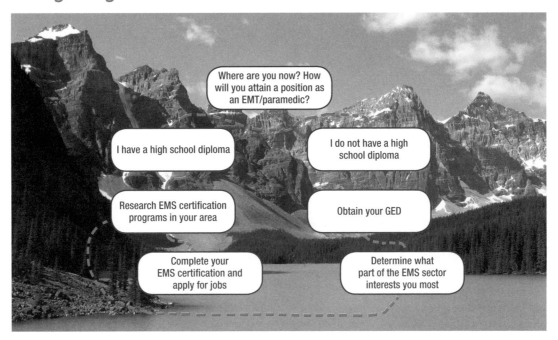

transportation for patients between medical facilities. Another good option is seeking work with a hospital, where you will be in charge of transporting critically injured patients to more specialized hospitals or trauma centers, all while keeping the patients' vital signs stable.

Scout the terrain. Certification is required before you can pursue a position as an entry-level EMT. This is for two specific reasons. First, a certification guarantees a minimum standard of care; and second, it protects you, the professional EMT or paramedic, from liability. Each state's requirements vary; however, once you are certified in one state, it is often possible to transfer that certification in the event of relocation. In order to become certified, you must enroll in a formal emergency medical technician training program. These are available at most community colleges. Check the colleges closest to you for information about application and enrollment. After approximately 35 sessions, you will be administered a written test (and sometimes a physical fitness assessment). Upon the receipt of a passing grade, you will be given your EMT-basic certification and may begin seeking employment.

Notes from the Field

Tim Walsh
EMT-Basic
Virginia Beach, Virginia

What were you doing before you decided to become an EMT?

I just had graduated from college with a history degree. I had always wanted to get involved in the emergency medical service sector, but was either too busy or just reluctant because I was not sure how I would handle dealing with death and suffering.

Why did you decide to pursue a career as an EMT?

I decided to work as an EMT while I finished my prerequisites for nursing school. The job gave me exposure to health care and solidified my interest in the field.

Find the path that's right for you. Determining where to best seek employment as an EMT or paramedic varies depending on where you live. If you live in a rural area, many of the emergency services may be staffed on a voluntary basis. In order to find a salaried position as an EMT, it may be necessary for you to work with nursing homes or other managed care facilities, or to join the staff of a hospital. In these types of positions, you are more likely to transport patients that are stabilized, which is appealing to many. However, if you live in a more metropolitan area, the likelihood of finding a paid position with the city as an EMT or paramedic is much greater.

Go back to school. To maintain your certification as an EMT-basic, you must recertify every two years. Your recertification is contingent upon holding a job in the emergency medical services. But why stop there? Instead of returning to school to recertify as an EMT-basic, enroll in the classes necessary to reach the EMT-intermediate and, finally, paramedic certification levels. By continuing your own education, you will not only demand a better salary and more senior positions, you will also be able to provide more comprehensive care to each of your patients.

What was involved in terms of education and training?

To become an EMT-basic I took a semester-long class with clinicals and then sat for a statewide exam. Once I was certified, I had to take a certain number of continuing education classes to maintain my certification.

What are the keys to success and the qualities of a good EMT?

The keys to success for an EMT are patience and knowledge. You need to be patient, because you are going to see a lot of frustrating things out on the street. You can become very jaded about how broken the American health care system is when dealing with many of the folks who call 911 (some on a regular basis.) You also need to be smart, and able to assess a whole situation to avoid getting tunnel vision with a patient. No two calls are ever the same and there are quite a few times when you will need to rely on "educated improvising."

Landmarks

If you are in your twenties . . . If you do not have a high school diploma, you should begin by obtaining your general equivalency diploma (GED). This is usually the minimum education requirement necessary in order to become certified as an EMT or paramedic. Almost all community colleges offer emergency medical service training programs. Research those nearby to find the best fit for you.

If you are in your thirties or forties . . . Career advancement and opportunities are best for those with advanced degrees. Consider returning to school to complete your bachelor's or master's degree. You may be able to obtain your EMT/paramedic certification simultaneous to your studies.

If you are in your fifties . . . If you are already employed in the health care or public service industry, you may be able to unite your current experience with some of the more specialized sectors of the EMT/paramedic position, such as state-certified instructor, dispatcher, or the sale and marketing of medical equipment.

If you are over sixty . . . Most states do not have an age limit on the certification of an EMT or paramedic. However, you should honestly assess your level of health, as a great deal of cardiovascular and muscular strength is required to do this type of work with success.

Further Resources

The **National Association of Emergency Medical Technicians (NAEMT)** represents emergency medical service practitioners. NAEMT serves through advocacy, educational programs, and research with membership reaching 25,000 in the United States. http://www.naemt.org

The **National Highway Traffic Safety Administration (NHTSA)** is a government database of laws, regulations, and safety operation of motor vehicles in the United States. The NHTSA maintains the Office of Emergency Medical Services. Their mission is to reduce accidental death and disability through coordinating comprehensive emergency medical services and 911 systems with the EMS community. http://www.nhtsa.dot.gov

The **National Registry of Emergency Medical Technicians (NREMT)** is a national certification agency for those employed in the emergency ambulance services sector. NREMT is responsible for maintaining the standards of qualification and testing of those who wish to work as an EMT or paramedic. Here you can locate exam sites, apply for recertification, and check the status of any individual working in the EMS field. http://www.nremt.org

Building Inspector

Building Inspector

Career Compasses

Guide yourself to a career as a building inspector.

Relevant Knowledge of building codes and violations (40%)

Communication Skills to convey issues to construction companies (20%)

Organizational Skills to keep detailed records of inspections (20%)

Mathematical Skills for reading and deciphering schematics and blueprints (20%)

Destination: Building Inspector

In the United States, all structures are regulated through a system of codes and ordinances designed to protect the people within these structures. Building inspectors are charged with confirming the safety of any structure or a single aspect of a structure, be it a home or commercial building, bridge, highway or other thruway, plumbing or water system, electrical grid, ventilation or ductwork layout, and many others. This is an ongoing process. An inspector will visit a job site during the earliest phases of construction and diligently return until that structure is complete and up to code. If problems are found, it is the building inspector's responsibility to notify the construction company of any violations and ensure that they are corrected.

Building inspectors generally travel to construction sites within their region. Often they work alone, but when assigned to a large-scale project they will team up with other inspectors in order to work more quickly and efficiently. A general building inspector checks the structural quality and safety of an entire building, from the blueprints all the way through the final walk-through. They even investigate the condition of the soil where the foundation will be poured. Though they are careful to look at every part of a structure, building inspectors are most concerned with fire safety. They focus on firewalls, exits, sprinklers, and smoke detectors. Sometimes, you will find exclusive fire safety inspectors working with a municipality's fire department, rather than with the public works department. Home inspection is a field similar to building inspection, but home inspectors are responsible for the safety and condition of residential rather than commercial structures. Public works inspectors are charged with the complete inspection of any municipal project, from sewer systems to highways and everything in between.

Essential Gear

Build up a tool kit. Although most inspections are done visually, inspectors sometimes must rely on tools to help them make an accurate determination of a structure's safety. From a simple tape measure to more complicated concrete strength measurers, an inspector has a number of options to help make their jobs not only easier, but also more accurate. You may want to purchase your own set of tools and familiarize yourself with them. Another item that many would-be inspectors would not immediately think of purchasing is a good digital camera: if you cannot make a code determination at the job site, you can take a photo to inspect more closely later, or to use in a consultation with someone more knowledgeable in that aspect of the construction.

General building inspectors often begin their careers with one specialization, and then branch out as they seek training in other fields. Some common single specializations are electrical, plumbing, elevator, and mechanical inspections—a frequent career path for those who were once employed in that sector of the construction field. They verify that all the work that falls under each heading was done properly. Certain parts of the country offer even more specializations. For example, in areas of the country where flooding, tornados, hurricanes, or other natural disasters are routine, there is a call for inspectors who are experts in the additional regulations in place to safeguard structures and their occupants from these incidents.

Essential Gear

Get in good shape. A construction site is muddy, dusty, and packed with building materials. It can be a dangerous place. Inspectors are expected to pick their way through these scenes and must go wherever the inspection takes them, be it up onto scaffolding or down into partially completed foundations. Being nimble on your feet and capable of squeezing into small places can only help your ability to perform the task well.

It is the responsibility of the inspector to preserve and implement all laws regarding the proper construction and use of a building, no matter what. This includes issuing building, work, and occupancy permits; enforcing construction and building codes; and maintaining comprehensive written reports on each job site. If a citation or stop work order is issued, the inspector will file the required paperwork and verify that the dangerous condition has been corrected before lifting those orders.

Every jurisdiction requires licensing and certification for all types of building inspectors. A would-be inspector must have a high school diploma in order to take the appropriate exams for a specific region. Some states require their inspectors to be licensed by the state. This license is maintained by performing a set number of inspections per year and by the licensee retaining his or her own liability insurance. Most inspectors choose to join an industry association affiliated with the type of inspection they wish to pursue. With this membership, inspectors can be assured of a wealth of certification, advancement, and employment opportunities.

The field of building inspection is expected to grow by more than 18 percent in the next 10 years. Despite the slowdown of the economy as of late, the infrastructure of the United States is continually aging. As it becomes necessary to repair these buildings, roads, and bridges, building inspectors will be called on to ensure that any work undertaken is being completed with an eye on the public's safety. Additionally, with the growing popularity of "green building," building inspectors that specialize in these new construction concepts and materials are almost guaranteed a plethora of employment opportunities. The most significant gains in sustainability can only be acquired if the construction team works from the ground up, with inspectors, architectural planners, and contractors pooling their knowledge to create a workable solution for helping to conserve the environment.

You Are Here

Set yourself on the path to becoming a building inspector.

Do you have an excellent eye for detail? At least a portion of every element of building inspection is done by sight. Even the best inspector's eyes will get a little weary. However, it is imperative that an inspector takes note of each nut, bolt, beam, and brace. Are you up to the task of working through a building piece by piece? Fortunately, most inspectors not only carry notebooks and cameras, they also have the use of devices such as laptops and personal organizers to ensure that nothing is missed. Inspectors employed as plan examiners and specification inspectors spend much of their day poring over blueprints to make sure that all work is done according to their specifications and code requirements.

Are you a first-rate communicator with personal integrity? Nearly all real estate developers are upright businessmen. But there can be a few who would not mind skirting a building code or two to save a few dollars. Building inspectors need to clearly convey any code infractions to the developer's foremen, so that they may be quickly and accurately corrected. Sometimes—especially if the foremen have been lax in accommodating regular inspections—it can be costly to re-do work that has gotten too far along to fix easily. Building inspectors must be firm and resolute in seeing that their citations are enforced. And they certainly should not be swayed by the offer of a little "cash advance" to look the other way. That could ultimately put not only their career in danger, but also the lives of the people who will be using that building day after day.

Would you prefer a standardized work schedule? Building inspectors are on the job during regular business hours. This makes this career a fine choice for someone with a family, or obligations that would not allow them to work nights or weekends. Occasionally, it becomes necessary that an inspector work longer hours than usual, especially if there is a sudden boom in construction within the region. Also, if there is an accident at a construction site, inspectors must report to the scene immediately in order to take a report and ascertain if the work can continue.

Organizing Your Expedition

Get everything in order as you prepare to become a building inspector.

Decide on a destination. Approximately 40 percent of building inspectors work for municipal building departments or a city agency. These inspectors are primarily responsible for commercial structures, bridges and tunnels, or any other public works construction. The most opportunities for these jobs lie in metropolitan areas, where there is large-scale economic growth. Most other building inspectors tend to be self-employed or work within architectural or engineering firms. These inspectors are generally hired by prospective homebuyers to inspect houses or apartments. They may also work on a contract-by-contract basis for real estate developers.

Scout the terrain. The majority of building inspectors do not have advanced degrees. However, most positions do require some prior experience in the construction field. A degree in a relevant area, such as engineering, math, or architecture, can often substitute for previous job experience. Many community colleges now offer associate's degrees in the various inspection specializations, most commonly building and home inspection, or construction technology. Research what is offered at your nearby community college. If you do not wish to complete a degree program, you can still pursue a career in building inspection. Still, individual courses in geometry and algebra, as well as technical drawing or blueprint reading, will be a welcome addition to your résumé. Most states also call for a certification in your chosen field of inspection, as well as additional training and testing once you choose a specialization.

Navigating the Terrain

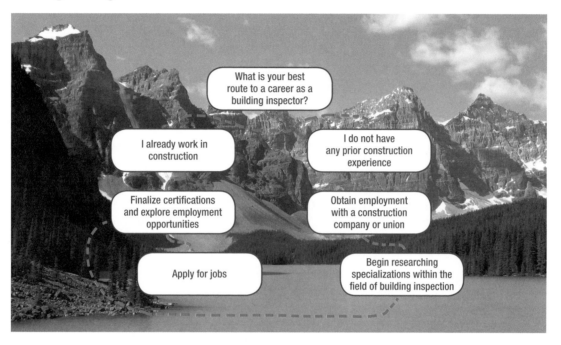

The International Code Council is an excellent resource that can help determine what requirements are specific to your region.

Find the path that's right for you. There are a host of specializations one can pursue as a building inspector. Home inspectors are responsible for investigating the interiors and exteriors of an entire residential structure and reporting the findings to an interested party, who will then use that information to make an informed bid on the property. Pursuing a position in home inspection necessitates a number of certifications, and is very susceptible to fluctuations in the housing market. One of the more popular specializations is public works. Because public works inspectors are certified to examine water and sewer systems; roadways and paving projects; bridges, tunnels, and dams; and structural steel, excavations, and concrete pouring, there is usually a variety of jobs to choose from—all falling under the jurisdiction of the local government. Specializations in electrical, plumbing, and mechanical systems (such as heating and ventilation), or appliance installation are also sought-after and positions tend to be widely available.

Notes from the Field
Brian Bosworth
Housing inspector/planning official
Woodbury, New Jersey

What were you doing before you decided to become a housing inspector?
I was working construction and taking some classes at Gloucester County College, the local community college.

Why did you decide to pursue a career as a housing inspector?
I heard that there was a job opening that would entail primarily field inspections and I thought it would be good experience. However, over the years, my primary job became performing housing inspections for sales and rentals, as well as the administrator for the combined planning/zoning board.

Landmarks

If you are in your twenties . . . The best opportunities are for those with some college experience, especially engineering or architectural training. Consider pursuing a college degree, then becoming certified as a plan inspector. This can allow you to pass over the hands-on component of construction and instead move directly into inspection.

If you are in your thirties or forties . . . Without much experience in the construction industry, becoming a building inspector can be difficult. If you do not have any comparable experience, it would be best to begin by obtaining work with a contractor or union. Build your knowledge of basic construction techniques and plan to move into the field of inspection after a few successful years.

If you are in your fifties . . . This can be an ideal age to begin a career in building inspection, especially if you have experience working in a compatible field. Your level of expertise in the field can lend the right touch of gravity when working to correct code violations with contractors and real estate developers.

What was involved in terms of education and training?

The New Jersey Department of Community Affairs has information on the various classes and tests required to become licensed. Besides a construction background, classes such as cost estimating and surveying are helpful.

What are the keys to success and the qualities of a good building inspector?

A thorough knowledge of the various building codes and the ability to work and communicate well with the public, contractors, and the governing body is very important. Continuing success relies on keeping up with the various code changes and interpretations.

If you are over sixty . . . If you have spent many years working in the construction field, moving into inspection is a natural progression. There is a fair amount of physical activity involved, but if you are in average shape, there should be no barrier to exploring work in this field.

Further Resources

If you would like more information about becoming a home inspector, there are two organizations that will be helpful: the American Society of Home Inspectors and the **National Association of Home Inspectors.** http://www.ashi.org and http://www.nahi.org

The **Environmental Protection Agency** offers a primer on green building, containing information on resource-efficient materials and construction techniques designed to help protect the environment. http://www.epa.gov/greenbuilding

The **International Association of Electrical Inspectors** is dedicated to providing information and training opportunities for those in the field of electrical inspection. http://iaepi.org

Visit the **International Code Council** for building codes, certification information, and employment opportunities. http://iccsafe.org

Park Ranger

Park Ranger

Career Compasses

Guide yourself to a career as a park ranger.

Relevant Knowledge of the natural environment of your assigned park (30%)

Caring about the ecosystem and the preservation of America's natural resources (30%)

Communication Skills to engage visitors and convey regulations, as well as work effectively with colleagues (30%)

Ability to Manage Stress to cope in emergency rescue or law enforcement situations (10%)

Destination: Park Ranger

From the cartoon antics of an agitated Ranger Smith chasing Yogi Bear and his illicit picnic basket through Jellystone Park to the grave warning that "only you can prevent forest fires" imparted by Smokey the Bear, the familiar and beloved images of park rangers ingrained in the American mind have inspired scores of children to dream of such a career. And with more than 76 million acres of national park lands under the jurisdiction of the United States, there is a need for qualified people to help preserve and protect our parks. A career as a park ranger can be very difficult to instigate, though, and it requires a level of dedication and perseverance uncommon to other public safety and law enforcement positions.

Park rangers have one duty—to maintain and protect the natural environment of the United States to preserve it for future generations. To this end, there are a variety of duties that a ranger can expect. On any day, a ranger may patrol the grounds of the park, investigate any complaints or seeking out those not complying with regulations, lead guests on a nature walk or historical tour of landmarks and features of the park, participate in a search and rescue mission, or handle routine maintenance duties. Because of this, park rangers are often sorted into different divisions, each responsible for one aspect of keeping the park running smoothly.

One of the most common of these divisions is that of law enforcement rangers, who act as the police force in the protected areas of the country. Licensed to carry firearms and make arrests, they are responsible for maintaining the peace and tranquility of the park through apprehension of poachers, correction of any safety concerns, or action in response to reports of fire. It is not uncommon for police officers to transition to positions as park rangers, especially in rural areas. This can be a very dangerous job. The Department of Justice reports that law enforcement rangers rank highest in number of assaults and homicides than any other federal law enforcement position. The consumption of alcohol by hikers and campers, the remoteness of the location, and the firearms carried by poachers all lend another dimension of danger to the life of a park ranger.

The second most common position for a park ranger is that of an interpreter. These are the rangers who provide information to visitors. This information can be practical—where to rent campsites, the most updated

Essential Gear

Wilderness supplies. Park rangers carry a myriad of equipment, all dependent on where they are stationed. This gear consists of a radio, cell phone, GPS unit, detailed maps and guidebooks, first aid kit, flashlight, knife, multi-tool, rope, shovel, axe, life preserver, fire extinguisher, extra fuel and water, tent, sleeping bag, handcuffs and other standard police equipment, and much more. If a park ranger works in a very isolated park, more personal survival equipment will be added. If stationed in a urban area, more law enforcement equipment is the norm. In any case, this equipment is there to guarantee that a park ranger is ready for anything.

weather forecast, or driving directions—or educational. Rangers who work as interpreters are responsible for providing guided tours or demonstrations of a historical, cultural, or ecological nature, or offer seminars intended to complement the instruction students are receiving in school. No matter what their primary responsibility in the park may be, all park rangers must be experts on the resources under their stewardship. If they are wearing the uniform, all rangers must be able to answer any variety of questions posed by visitors with familiarity and authority.

Park rangers may hold a number of other positions in a national park, such as park guards. Park guards are in charge of making sure gates are locked, taking roads in and out of use due to varying seasonal conditions, and making certain that visitors have not strayed into unauthorized areas of the park. Emergency response teams are made up of park rangers who are skilled in wilderness first aid and are responsible for locating lost persons within the park. Some handle fire spotting and fighting, acting as the first line of response until a team of firefighters can arrive. Dispatchers answer emergency calls, and direct the appropriate team of park rangers or other law enforcement to the scene. There are also positions available in maintenance and administration, making sure all behind-the-scenes responsibilities to the park are met.

Essential Gear

Are these boots made for walking? They had better be. Park rangers work in all conditions and on all types of terrain. A comfortable, supportive pair of hiking boots will quickly become any new park ranger's favorite article of clothing. Invest in a pair of well-made, waterproof boots. Despite the initial expense, some reputable boot companies offer complimentary resoling and repair for the life of the boot.

The majority of park rangers are employed by the federal and state government through the National Park Service or the state park systems. However, there is immense competition for those positions, especially for permanent placement. Only aspiring park rangers who have already proved themselves thoroughly dedicated to pursuing this career tend to make the cut. These days most park rangers have a high level of education and some degree of experience. A typical park ranger may have a bachelor's degree in earth science coupled with a minor in law enforcement, or he or she may have worked as a volunteer with a conservation effort while attending college. Law enforcement park rangers also must attend a seasonal law enforcement training program (SLETP) consisting of 334 class hours. There, students learn how to use firearms, investigate crimes, and handle the other enforcement aspects of the position. After successful completion, a prospective ranger is then able to accept any commission that might be offered once a physical and drug screening are passed. Because of the extra training required, there is more job availability in this area of the field.

Most park rangers work as seasonal employees. During off-months, they may obtain employment as hunting or fishing guides, or in private security. Some work for private parks or campgrounds. There is quite a lot of growth available to a park ranger. From the entry-level position, rangers can expect to be promoted to district rangers, park managers, or staff specialists.

From the rocky coastline of Maine to the majesty of the Grand Canyon to lush forests of the Pacific Northwest, the life of a park ranger can be one of breathtaking beauty. But the demand to play a role in the preservation of America's natural resources is high. Preparing to become a park ranger requires dedication, as these are highly coveted positions. But as famed conservationist John Muir once said, "Everybody needs beauty as well as bread." A park ranger is lucky enough to get both at once.

You Are Here

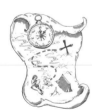

Set yourself on the path to becoming a park ranger.

Do you have a love of the outdoors? A park ranger's main responsibility is protecting and preserving the natural resources in the park to which he or she is assigned. To this end, it is a must that aspiring rangers have a high level of respect for the natural environment. They should be able to set an example at all times to those visiting the park. The conditions in which the rangers patrol can be highly changeable. A park ranger is responsible for completing their duties no matter what the temperature, conditions, or terrain.

Are you comfortable working on your own and handling the unexpected? The majority of a park ranger's time is spent patrolling the park to which he or she is assigned. This is sometimes done in a vehicle customized to the terrain of the park, but is often done on foot. Many spend their time making their rounds alone. Because of this, a park ranger should be able to work on an unstructured schedule, taking the time to investigate anything suspicious in a self-directed fashion. Occasionally, they will need to search out wayward hikers, apprehend poachers, or stave off wild animals. In exceptionally sprawling parks, help may not be readily available. A ranger must call on his or her law enforcement and wilderness training in order to determine the correct course of action and execution.

Do you enjoy dealing with the public? Many Americans utilize the national park system to escape from their daily grind. However, just as many are unfamiliar with the rules and regulations that are in place to help preserve these parks and forests. If a park ranger discovers visitors violating any of the park rules inadvertently, it is their duty to correct the behavior. Doing so can be a delicate matter. A park ranger does not want to discourage any visitor from returning to the park, but must project authority, so the way in which he or she speaks to the public is important. Park rangers may also regularly give talks and tours to visitors. Having an easy way with the public can make the experience more enjoyable for all.

Navigating the Terrain

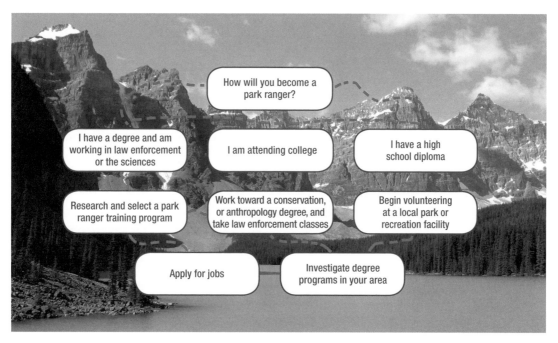

Notes from the Field

Cris Sanguino
Superintendent II (also known as captain), California State Parks
Borrego Springs, California

What were you doing before you decided to become a park ranger?

I began my state park career in 1979 in a school program called Youth Conservation Corps. It was a program in high school designed to give students a well-rounded view of all aspects of the agency while providing environmental education to us. We also spent the majority of time building trails in parks. We received school credit for this program as well as being paid ($1.77 per hour!).

After graduation, I was offered a job cleaning restrooms and picking up trash on beaches in Santa Cruz. Being 17 years old and looking at community college, I accepted this seasonal position. It led to permanent civil service in various maintenance positions. The maintenance and trades offered many classes to train me in skills such as electrical, plumbing, and carpentry. I also chose to pursue a specialty in water and wastewater treatment operations. I spent a total of nine years in maintenance and trades.

Why did you decide to pursue a career as a park ranger?

During the years of being in maintenance, I had several mentors from both the maintenance classifications and the ranger classification. Some of my mentors had become rangers after working several years in maintenance. There had been a program in place to make it possible for non-peace officers to become peace officers by waiving the two-year educational requirement and substitute job experience. In the 1980s it was called the Field Trainee Program, but it only lasted three years and I was not able to take advantage of it at that time.

After working at Natural Bridges State Beach, I became interested in the education portion of the ranger classification. I put myself through docent training and began doing public tours. I also participated in many interpretive events within the parks. In 1989, the Field Trainee Program was reinvented as the Field Cadet Program, because many people within the department (including myself) had been asking where this program had gone. When the Field Cadet Program was approved, they waived half of the educational requirements and interviewed 60 people for two positions. I was able to get one of the two positions.

So to synopsize this long story, I decided to change my career because I became interested in the educational programs and resource protection aspects of a park ranger. I felt I could be a good peace officer and I was (and still am) very interested in the public interaction aspects of the job.

What was involved in terms of education and training?

The field cadet position required 40 college units instead of the 60 college units [usually] required. Job experience was substituted for college in my case, and this was a very unique opportunity that had not been offered since 1989. I have since gathered my 60+ units. The academy in 1989 was 840 hours long and today I think it is still around the same length. Sadly, the field cadet opportunities no longer exist.

What are the keys to success and the qualities of a good park ranger?

Being interested in the role and history of park rangers is paramount! I feel that so many rangers forget that we impact how future generations feel about their surrounding environment and resources. They must be familiar with the park's resources in the first place. This is a huge topic that is not included in the academy. I also expect staff to recognize how to protect our resources, whether it is through the fish and game code, fire code, or [state codes of regulation] Be [it] burl poaching, Native American artifact protection, illegal wood-cutting, or illegal taking of fish and game, this is the most important reason we are here.

Staff should also prevent people from injuring themselves by making safety contacts. At the ocean or in the mountains or desert, rangers know how people get hurt! It is a big part of our job to protect them by talking to them about their activities and how to prevent injuries. We are law enforcement, and we are expected to recognize crimes and prevent crime from occurring. This relates to the many domestic disputes, gang issues, drugs, and other non-resource related crime. I expect my staff to be able to handle any one of these situations. There is a section in our departmental manual that reads what out main goals as State Park Peace Officers are. Section 1301 (B) reads:

In general, there are three priorities within the role of safety and enforcement:

(1) Protect people from people.
(2) Protect people from parks.
(3) Protect parks from people. *(continued on page 88)*

Notes from the Field

(continued from page 87)

I still fall back on this section when deciding on when to act.

Finally, I feel that another key to success would be to know how to make the public's visit an enjoyable one. Talk to children! Think of them as future rangers. Spark their interests with a story about being a park ranger. Make them want to come back!

What surprised you the most about your role as a park ranger?

What I have seen the role evolve into has surprised me! I have seen the role as an educator turn into an entire separate classification as a "state park interpreter." I have seen the role of resource manager turn into the classification of "resource scientist."

I have seen the administrative functions such as accounting, purchasing, and attendance reporter grow without district support. And I have seen the role of the state park ranger turn into a state park peace officer. I understand that we have peace officer duties and high crime areas within the system. Trust me, I have worked in some high crime areas and I was also assigned to a department of justice narcotics task force during my career. I also understand that the term *peace officer* in our title was necessary. In my opinion this change was not intended to make us 100 percent police, it was to get the attention of the voters and legislators to understand that we do perform law enforcement duties. I do not believe that it was intended to take away our function of being resource protectors, educators, and guardians of our historic and cultural artifacts.

Organizing Your Expedition

Get everything in order as you prepare to become a park ranger.

Decide on a destination. No matter where in the country you may live, there is sure to be a national or state park nearby. However, only nine schools across the country offer the required SLETP training to become a law enforcement park ranger. You have to determine whether or not you are willing to travel to receive the additional training required of law enforcement park rangers. It is also very desirable for a prospective park ranger to have an advanced degree. You may want to select a college based in the location you are most interested in serving. That way, you can tailor your schooling to represent the natural environment of that area of the country.

Scout the terrain. Most rangers are employed by the National Park Service, which has a comprehensive Web site that features openings throughout the country. While you are seeking employment, it is helpful to volunteer at either a local park or other natural attractions such as zoos or botanical gardens. The National Park Service offers their own volunteer program called Volunteers-in-Parks. By volunteering your time, you can not only enhance your skill set, but you will also meet a number of working park rangers who may be able to help you seek employment opportunities, or give you an insider's look at the business of being a ranger.

Find the path that's right for you. Park rangers work in urban, suburban, and rural areas. What type of environment are you most interested in? Rescue work is certainly exciting, but in New York's Central Park, there is less danger of getting lost than losing your wallet to an enterprising pickpocket. Park rangers in metropolitan areas act as a police force within the park, and in fact partner with law enforcement when necessary. In rural areas, a park ranger is much more of a conservationist. However, there you will also encounter more catastrophic accidents—the wilderness can be dangerous when hikers and campers are unprepared. Parks located in suburban areas have a more educational bent to them—park rangers there tend to work with visiting students often. Also, if you have a particular interest in history, you could search for placement at one of the hundreds of historical sites protected by the state and federal governments. Because there are so many different landscapes in the United States—mountains, plains, beaches, and deserts—it should not be difficult to select the environment that fits you best.

Landmarks

If you are in your twenties . . . It is possible to work as a seasonal park ranger without a college education, but if you are serious about gaining a permanent position in the field, it is necessary to complete a bachelor's degree, specifically in earth science, natural resource management, anthropology, or any other program of study related to the conservation of the earth's resources. A minor in law enforcement can signal to an employer that you are serious about this career path.

If you are in your thirties or forties . . . The maximum age of entry for most park rangers is 37. If you are over that age, it is still feasible to work within the national park system as an interpreter—contextualizing the features of the park to enrich a visitor's experience. These tend to be seasonal positions, however, and most interpreters must re-apply for their position each year.

Essential Gear

Go team! The National Park Service values teamwork between their rangers above all else. In fact, park rangers, no matter what their rank, all wear exactly the same uniform. Why? Because it fosters a sense of camaraderie. Work to cultivate a bond between all of the park rangers. Not only will it make the workplace a enjoyable place to work, but it will instill a sense of trust that can be badly needed when in an emergency situation.

If you are in your fifties . . . If you are interested in a wilderness career and live in an area with abundant natural features that are a draw to tourists, check the job boards at your local chamber of commerce. Many resort areas hire guides for their guests' convenience. A job as a hunting, fishing, rafting, or skiing guide may be a perfect fit, especially if you have special experience in one of those areas.

If you are over sixty . . . Oftentimes private companies based in rural areas have a need for security guards, especially logging companies. Private campgrounds also hire staff to collect payments and help to ensure the safety of their guests. If you have previously held a position in a science-related field, it is also worthwhile to check into the local zoos, aquariums, botanical gardens, or arboretums. These sites often have a staff of tour guides on hand to give talks and tours to visitors, and this type of position can satisfy a wish of working outdoors.

Further Resources

Adopt-a-Ranger is a worldwide initiative to supply much-needed park rangers to developing countries. http://www.adopt-a-ranger.org

The **Association of National Park Rangers (ANPR)** is a professional organization dedicated to promoting the stewardship of preserved parklands through education, training, and public advocacy. They offer employments listings, mentoring programs, and career-enhancing seminars and workshops to park rangers of all levels. http://www.anpr.org

The **National Park Service** oversees the conservation of the federally-sponsored parks in the United States. Its Web site includes information about the locations of parks and rules and regulations for visitors, as well as career opportunities and training requirement information. http://www.nps.gov

The mission of the **National Recreation and Park Association (NRPA)** is "to advance parks, recreation and environmental conservation efforts that enhance the quality of life for all people" through education, certification opportunities, and advocacy. http://www.nrpa.org

Park Law Enforcement Association (PLEA) offers support and professional development to park rangers through employment listings, discussion boards, and newsletters. http://www.parkranger.com

Parole Officer

Parole Officer

Career Compasses

Guide yourself to a career as a parole officer.

Relevant knowledge of correctional practices, state and federal laws pertaining to criminal justice, and community and state agencies and resources (30%)

Communication Skills to begin and maintain a positive rapport with clients (30%)

Organizational Skills to handle a large number of cases at one time (20%)

Ability to Manage Stress to cope with potential dangerous situations with criminal offenders (20%)

Destination: Parole Officer

A career as a parole officer can be one of the toughest, and one of the most fulfilling, paths one can choose. For every breakdown in the system, there are many more stories of ex-convicts who have become productive and law-abiding citizens, thanks in part to the guidance and support of their parole officer. And with each success, one who has embarked on this journey will feel an immense sense of pride—and relief—that they were able to save another from a life that would surely lead to a dead end.

Anyone convicted of a crime in the United States will eventually come under the authority of a parole officer, whether they spend time in prison or are immediately placed on probation. The duty of a parole officer is to discourage these offenders from continuing on their previous path and instead encourage them to take a proactive position to change for the better. Most of this supervision is done through personal contact with an offender and his or her family, usually on-site at a home or workplace. Occasionally it may take place in the offices of therapists and counselors who also work with the client. A small number of parole officers work exclusively in an office setting with clients, but this is rare these days.

Essential Gear

Sharpen your pencil. Writing accurate and in-depth pre-sentence reports are a major part of the daily responsibilities of a parole officer. These reports are the foundation of the court's sentencing decisions, and are utilized by the parole board to determine whether or not an offender is ready to be released. They must contain all relevant information about an offender and the crimes they have committed, as well as the parole officer's personal recommendations as to whether or not the person in question is ready for release and suggestions for post-incarceration counseling and rehabilitation. Parole officer Stacey Pace agrees: "I was surprised by the amount of written reports that probation and parole officers are required to prepare. I remember a college professor lecturing in one of my community corrections classes that if we did not know how to write, we better learn fast because if we get a job in this field, we were going to be doing it a lot! He was right!"

Because parole officers are in essence a part of the law enforcement field, a large component of their responsibility is both pretrial and pre-release investigations of the 20 to 100 offenders under their authority. When an offender has been charged with a crime, the assigned parole officer will study any previous reports, a psychological profile, and any criminal record. Some prisoners do not pose a threat to the general public and can be sentenced to probation, or released on their own recognizance while awaiting trial. Others, who are violent, repeat offenders, must be immediately jailed. The report of a parole officer is the single most important piece of evidence to help the court determine how the prisoner should be treated within the judicial system.

When a prisoner has shown promising behavior while incarcerated and becomes eligible for release, the parole officer will again step in with a recommended rehabilitation plan for the offender. Once on probation, the parole officer helps the offender put this plan into effect and encourages follow-through with regular meetings, the request of assistance from a client's family and friends, and the utilization of community groups and religious institutions with which a client may be affiliated. Some offenders may be required to wear an electronic tracking device, which allows a parole officer to closely monitor a client's movements, or to take random drug tests, which a parole officer will administer. Parole officers can never forget that their clients are often violent offenders who cannot be wholly trusted. However, most offenders genuinely want to change for the better, and will comply with their parole officer's recommendations for treatment.

Essential Gear

Firearms training. Parole officers are often required to carry a weapon. In most states, they also must undergo at least forty hours of firearms training. It can also be beneficial to enroll in a self-defense course in order to learn how to protect yourself from harm in the event of a confrontation—without having to resort to using a gun.

There are a few types of parole officers one can aspire to become, though the job descriptions do tend to overlap. Parole officers supervise offenders who have been released from prison. Probation officers work with those who have been remanded to probation without a prison term. These roles often overlap with pretrial services officers, who focus on investigating offenders and creating pretrial reports. There are also correctional treatment specialists, who either work within the prison system to evaluate inmates and prepare them for parole, or outside the system to assist clients as they are released from parole. They liaison with the community to help initialize an action plan for the client by setting up employment and any necessary counseling or support groups.

Parole officers are required to have at least four years of college, culminating in a bachelor's degree. Fortunately, it does not require that the degree be targeted toward a law enforcement field. Many parole officers at least hold degrees in social work, psychology, or behavioral science, but just as often someone with training in an unrelated field can easily transition into the industry. Aspiring parole officers are then required to complete the training program offered by the state or federal government, depending on the desired career path, and pass a certification exam. It is also compulsory to pass an oral, psychological, and physical examination, as well as a drug screening. Some regions require firearms training. Once a parole officer is employed, there is generally a one-year probationary period that must be completed. Because many states are revising their mandatory sentencing guidelines and placing more emphasis on rehabilitation and alternate punishments, many offenders who would have spent years in prison are now being placed on probation. This will ensure that there will be exceptional employment growth in the field of probation, as well as good opportunities for advancement, especially in urban areas where the crime rates tend to scale higher than in rural areas.

You Are Here

Set yourself on the path to becoming a parole officer.

Are you empathetic, yet decisive? Sob stories, missed appointments, flimsy excuses, refusal to work, and, at worst, the commission of another crime—these are common roadblocks thrown before a parole officer while tending to an offender. Of course no offender wants to violate parole requirements and return to prison, but lacking the support of family and community, he or she may miss the required meetings in favor of hanging around with friends. Providing support to each client in the form of listening and relating to their daily obstacles can go a long way in inspiring a client to stay out of trouble. When a situation becomes hopeless, a parole officer cannot lack the courage to make the difficult decision of remanding an offender to prison, despite any protest from the client or any affection the parole officer may have for him or her.

Are you able to handle high-stress environments? Parole officers work with criminal offenders, who can be erratic at the very least, and sometimes dangerous. Add to that an overwhelming workload and a string of unremitting court dates. Needless to say, the numerous responsibilities of a parole officer make this career one of the most challenging out there. However, those who are able to manage well in a high-pressure environment report that working as a parole officer is highly satisfying, especially as they watch members of their communities leave their transgressions behind and go on to rewarding lives of their own.

Navigating the Terrain

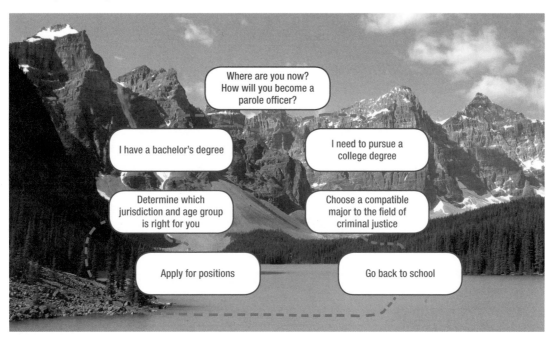

Where are you now? How will you become a parole officer?

I have a bachelor's degree

I need to pursue a college degree

Determine which jurisdiction and age group is right for you

Choose a compatible major to the field of criminal justice

Apply for positions

Go back to school

Do you have excellent communication skills? A parole officer spends most of the time counseling offenders. Because of this, parole officer is not a career for anyone with a retiring personality. Instead, you will want to be immediately open, friendly, and considerate to each client. Optimistically, this will lead a client to act in kind. The more quickly you can have frank conversations with each client, the easier it will become to get each individual the required help.

Organizing Your Expedition

Get everything in order as you prepare to become a parole officer.

Decide on a destination. There are two decisions to be made when pursuing a career as a parole officer. The first is whether you would you prefer to work in the federal jurisdictions or the state or local jurisdictions in your region. The majority of the jobs are to be found at the state

Notes from the Field

Stacey Pace
Probation/parole officer II, State of Montana
    Department of Corrections
Bozeman, Montana

What were you doing before you decided to become a parole officer?

I knew that I wanted to get into the community corrections business, but I had an assistant volleyball coaching job lined up, so upon graduation from college, I began that job. While doing that job, I obtained a part-time job at a pre-release center (for males and females). The pre-release housed both inmates and what they called "diversions," which were probationers. The easiest way to describe it is similar to a half-way house. I worked there for one and a half years, until several state probation/parole officer jobs became available. I applied and was offered a job in the Bozeman Adult Probation/Parole Office.

Why did you decide to pursue a career as a parole officer?

I have always been a people person and have an interest in helping others. I also enjoy hearing people's life stories, finding out where they came from and the circumstances and choices in their lives that have brought them to the point that they are in the criminal justice system. I was naïve to the realities of community corrections, but once I jumped in, I was even more intrigued. I am a believer that with few exceptions, you always have a choice. The choices may not be the best, but if you keep picking the best option, eventually, you will be making choices between two positives.

What was involved in terms of education and training?

I received a bachelor's degree in sociology, with an emphasis in criminal justice. I do not believe the state of Montana requires a specific bachelor's degree, as I know of officers with a bachelor's degree in other areas, but they do prefer some sort of bachelor's degree. My degree allowed me some insight into community corrections because I took classes specifically geared toward that, such as probation and parole, community corrections, criminal theory, [and] social psychology.

What are the keys to success and the qualities of a good parole officer?

Some of the qualities I believe make a good probation/parole officer are:

☞ Someone who is levelheaded, has common sense, and uses logic. The populations we work with often tend to be the opposite, so you have to keep your head and be reasonable.

☞ An effective communicator, an active listener, and an attentive observer. Communication requires both speaking and listening. In order to effect change, you have to understand where the other person is coming from and be able to explain your expectation on their level. Also, there are a lot of non-verbal cues that can give a PPO an idea as to what is going on. You can tell a lot just by observing behaviors.

☞ Good written communication skills. We write a lot of reports, which are viewed by judges, attorneys, victims, offenders, the public, and others, so it is a crucial part of our duties.

☞ A team player and supporter of the organization. We rely on each other a lot, and it is important to know someone has your back.

☞ Someone with integrity, good morals, and ethical standards.

☞ Someone who can see the short- and long-term goals of the department.

☞ Flexibility is a must. Often times I start out the day with a list and by the end of the day, I may have only gotten to one or two things on the list because other things come up.

☞ Organize/Prioritize. We often have many "irons in the fire," so to use a saying from one of my previous supervisors: "There are glass balls and rubber balls, our goal is to know which is which." Some things require immediate attention, while others can simmer for a bit and that can change in the blink of an eye.

What surprised you the most about your role as a parole officer?

One thing that surprised me is the extent to which PPO's get involved with offenders and their families. In order to help or guide people, you need to know where they come from. Our jobs involve social work and enforcement. It is an interesting combination and finding a balance can be challenging.

or local level. This is because the state prison systems are much more extensive than that of the federal government. It is also worth repeating that the majority of these positions will be found in urban areas—exactly where you will encounter higher wages, as well. The second choice you must make is whether you would prefer to work with adults or minors. The number of jobs available to those who work with adults is greater, but perhaps you relate well to adolescents and would be more fulfilled counseling that age group.

Scout the terrain. Training programs are offered by both the federal and state governments. Contact the department of corrections for your state. There you can find a list of available positions, all of which should indicate what type of instruction is required. In most areas, once a bachelor's degree is obtained, parole officers must attend a basic training program (usually four weeks in length) and 40 hours of firearms training. It is also worth noting that many new parole officers are also on probation—they must complete their first year before becoming full-fledged officers. Also, familiarize yourself with state and federal laws governing probation and parole issues, in your region as well as those surrounding. Study up on case management skills and counseling techniques. A working knowledge of recovery programs offered within the community is also helpful.

Essential Gear

Cellular phone, pager, or PDA. Parole officers are on-call 24 hours a day, and often must work nights and weekends. Some regions require that parole officer's live within 30 minutes of their workplace, so that they can be available to their clients at any time. Be sure your schedule is flexible enough to accommodate these kinds of fluctuations. Purchase a reliable cellular phone, pager, or PDA if one is not provided for you. Keep it charged and at the ready.

Find the path that's right for you. There are two completely divergent reasons why parole officer is an excellent long-term career choice at this time. First, many states have very strict three-strike mandatory sentencing guidelines. Despite the commission of less-serious non-violent crimes, repeat offenders are finding themselves serving lengthy prison terms. Many offenders become repeat offenders, and jails are filling quickly. Conversely, some areas of the country are investigating rehabilitation rather than punishment, granting offenders probation or compulsory terms in halfway houses or other programs as a last-ditch effort to keep them out of prison. This requires more officers to be assigned to the agencies that maintain these facilities.

Landmarks

If you are in your twenties . . . Applicants must be older than 21 and all parole officer positions require at least a four-year degree. The major you choose is up to you; however, social work, psychology, or communications can be very helpful, especially when paired with a few courses in criminal justice or law enforcement. Find a college that is a good fit for you and prepare for enrollment.

If you are in your thirties or forties . . . Federal parole officers cannot apply for positions once they pass the age of 37, but state parole officers often have no such restrictions. With a bachelor's degree and some prior work experience, you are an excellent candidate for a parole officer position. Prepare your résumé and begin searching for jobs.

If you are in your fifties . . . Use your past career, especially if it was within law enforcement, drug and alcohol counseling, or psychology, to move into the position of parole officer. Most agencies offer many levels of parole officers, including supervisory titles. Your previous experience may allow you to begin your new career in a higher post than any other applicant.

If you are over sixty . . . Because of the physical and mental stress that is a part of any parole officer position, it will be difficult but not impossible to obtain work in this field. If you have an advanced degree and years of applicable experience in law enforcement or counseling, you may have more luck looking for a position as a correctional treatment specialist. These specialists create rehabilitation plans tailored to each offender's requirements. Parole officers can then oversee an offender's compliance with these plans.

Further Resources

The **American Correctional Association (ACA)** is the resource for professional development in the field of corrections. http://www.aca.org

The **American Probation and Parole Association (APPA)** is the international association for those who serve in a professional capacity with probation, parole, and community-based rehabilitation at all levels of government. http://www.appa-net.org

The **National Council on Crime and Delinquency** promotes criminal justice reform to reduce the crime and delinquency in adults and children. http://www.nccd-crc.org

Appendix A

Going Solo: Starting Your Own Business

Starting your own business can be very rewarding—not only in terms of potential financial success, but also in the pleasure derived from building something from the ground up, contributing to the community, being your own boss, and feeling reasonably in control of your fate. However, business ownership carries its own obligations—both in terms of long hours of hard work and new financial and legal responsibilities. If you succeed in growing your business, your responsibilities only increase. Many new business owners come in expecting freedom only to find themselves chained tighter to their desks than ever before. Still, many business owners find greater satisfaction in their career paths than do workers employed by others.

The Internet has also changed the playing field for small business owners, making it easier than ever before to strike out on your own. While small mom-and-pop businesses such as hairdressers and grocery stores have always been part of the economic landscape, the Internet has made reaching and marketing to a niche easier and more profitable. This has made possible a boom in *microbusinesses*. Generally, a microbusiness is considered to have under ten employees. A microbusiness is also sometimes called a *SOHO* for "small office/home office."

The following appendix is intended to explain, in general terms, the steps in launching a small business, no matter whether it is selling your Web-design services or opening a pizzeria with business partners. It will also point out some of the things you will need to bear in mind. Remember also that the particular obligations of your municipality, state, province, or country may vary, and that this is by no means a substitute for doing your own legwork. Further suggested reading is listed at the end.

Crafting a Business Plan

It has often been said that success is 1 percent inspiration and 99 percent perspiration. However, the interface between the two can often be hard to achieve. The first step to taking your idea and making it reality is constructing a viable *business plan*. The purpose of a business plan is to think things all the way through, to make sure your ideas really are profitable, and to figure out the "who, what, when, where, why, and how" of your business. It fills in the details for three areas: your goals, why you think they are attainable, and how you plan to get to there. "You need to know where you're going before you take that first step," says Drew Curtis, successful Internet entrepreneur and founder of the popular newsfilter Fark.com.

Take care in writing your business plan. Generally, these documents contain several parts: An *executive summary* stating the essence of the plan; a *market summary* explaining how a need exists for the product and service you will supply and giving an idea of potential profitability by comparing your business to similar organizations; a *company description* which includes your products and services, why you think your organization will succeed, and any special advantages you have, as well as a description of *organization* and *management*; and your *marketing and sales strategy*. This last item should include market highlights and demographic information and trends that relate to your proposal. Also include a *funding request* for the amount of start-up capital you will need. This is supported by a section on *financials*, or the sort of cash flow you can expect, based on market analysis, projection, and comparison with existing companies. Other needed information, such as personal financial history, résumés, legal documents, or pictures of your product, can be placed in *appendices*.

Use your business plan to get an idea of how much startup money is necessary and to discipline your thinking and challenge your preconceived notions before you develop your cash flow. The business plan will tell you how long it will take before you turn a profit, which in turn is linked to how long it will before you will be able to pay back investors or a bank loan—which is something that anyone supplying you with money will want to know. Even if you are planning to subsist on grants or you are not planning on investment or even starting a for-profit company, the discipline imposed by the business plan is still the first step to organizing your venture.

A business plan also gives you a realistic view of your personal financial obligations. How long can you afford to live without regular income? How are you going to afford medical insurance? When will your business begin turning a profit? How much of a profit? Will you need to reinvest your profits in the business, or can you begin living off of them? Proper planning is key to success in any venture.

A final note on business plans: Take into account realistic expected profit minus realistic costs. Many small business owners begin by underestimating start-ups and variable costs (such as electricity bills), and then underpricing their product. This effectively paints them into a corner from which it is hard to make a profit. Allow for realistic market conditions on both the supply and the demand side.

Partnering Up

You should think long and hard about the decision to go into business with a partner (or partners). Whereas other people can bring needed capital, expertise, and labor to a business, they can also be liabilities. The questions you need to ask yourself are:

☞ Will this person be a full and equal partner? In other words, are they able to carry their own weight? Make a full and fair assessment of your potential partner's personality. Going into business with someone who lacks a work ethic, or prefers giving directions to working in the trenches, can be a frustrating experience.

☞ What will they contribute to the business? For instance, a partner may bring in start-up money, facilities, or equipment. However, consider if this is enough of a reason to bring them on board. You may be able to get the same advantages in another way—for instance, renting a garage rather than working out of your partner's. Likewise, doubling skill sets does not always double productivity.

☞ Do they have any liabilities? For instance, if your prospective partner has declared bankruptcy in the past, this can hurt your collective venture's ability to get credit.

☞ Will the profits be able to sustain all the partners? Many start-up ventures do not turn profits immediately, and what little they do produce can be spread thin amongst many partners. Carefully work out the math.

Also bear in mind that going into business together can put a strain on even the best personal relationships. No matter whether it is family, friends, or strangers, keep everything very professional with written agreements regarding these investments. Get everything in writing, and be clear where obligations begin and end. "It's important to go into business with the right people," says Curtis. "If you don't—if it degrades into infighting and petty bickering—it can really go south quickly."

Incorporating. . . or Not

Think long and hard about incorporating. Starting a business often requires a fairly large—and risky—financial investment, which in turn exposes you to personal liability. Furthermore, as your business grows, so does your risk. Incorporating can help you shield yourself from this liability. However, it also has disadvantages.

To begin with, incorporating is not necessary for conducting professional transactions such as obtaining bank accounts and credit. You can do this as a sole proprietor, partnership, or simply by filing a DBA ("doing business as") statement with your local court (also known as "trading as" or an "assumed business name"). The DBA is an accounting entity that facilitates commerce and keeps your business' money separate from your own. However, the DBA does not shield you from responsibility if your business fails. It is entirely possible to ruin your credit, lose your house, and have your other assets seized in the unfortunate event of bankruptcy.

The purpose of incorporating is to shield yourself from personal financial liability. In case the worst happens, only the business' assets can be taken. However, this is not always the best solution. Check your local laws: Many states have laws that prevent a creditor from seizing a non-incorporated small business' assets in case of owner bankruptcy. If you are a corporation, however, the things you use to do business that are owned by the corporation—your office equipment, computers, restaurant refrigerators, and other essential equipment—may be seized by creditors, leaving you no way to work yourself out of debt. This is why it is imperative to consult with a lawyer.

There are other areas in which being a corporation can be an advantage, such as business insurance. Depending on your business needs, insurance can be for a variety of things: malpractice, against delivery failures or spoilage, or liability against defective products or accidents. Furthermore, it is easier to hire employees, obtain credit, and buy health insurance as an organization than as an individual. However, on the downside, corporations are subject to specific and strict laws concerning management and ownership. Again, you should consult with a knowledgeable legal expert.

Among the things you should discuss with your legal expert are the advantages and disadvantages of incorporating in your jurisdiction and which type of incorporation is best for you. The laws on liability and how much of your profit will be taken away in taxes vary widely by state and country. Generally, most small businesses owners opt for *limited liability companies* (LLCs), which gives them more control and a more flexible management structure. (Another possibility is a *limited liability partnership*, or *LLP*, which is especially useful for professionals such as doctors and lawyers.) Finally, there is the *corporation*, which is characterized by transferable ownerships shares, perpetual succession, and, of course, limited liability.

Most small businesses are sole proprietorships, partnerships, or privately-owned corporations. In the past, not many incorporated, since it was necessary to have multiple owners to start a corporation. However, this is changing, since it is now possible in many states for an individual to form a corporation. Note also that the form your business takes is usually not set in stone: A sole proprietorship or partnership can switch to become an LLC as it grows and the risks increase; furthermore, a successful LLC can raise capital by changing its structure to become a corporation and selling stock.

Legal Issues

Many other legal issues besides incorporating (or not) need to be addressed before you start your business. It is impossible to speak directly to every possible business need in this brief appendix, since regulations, licenses, and health and safety codes vary by industry and locality. A restaurant in Manhattan, for instance, has to deal not only with the usual issues such as health inspectors, and the state liquor board, but obscure regulations such as New York City's cabaret laws, which prohibit dancing without a license in a place where alcohol is sold. An asbestos-abatement company, on the other hand, has a very different set of standards it has to abide by, including federal regulations. Researching applicable laws is part of starting up any business.

Part of being a wise business owner is knowing when you need help. There is software available for things like bookkeeping, business plans, and Web site creation, but generally, consulting with a knowledgeable professional—an accountant or a lawyer (or both)—is the smartest move. One of the most common mistakes is believing that just because you have expertise in the technical aspects of a certain field, you know all about running a business in that field. Whereas some people may balk at the expense, by suggesting the best way to deal with possible problems, as well as cutting through red tape and seeing possible pitfalls that you may not even have been aware of, such professionals usually more than make up for their cost. After all, they have far more experience at this than does a first-time business owner!

Financial

Another necessary first step in starting a business is obtaining a bank account. However, having the account is not as important as what you do with it. One of the most common problems with small businesses is undercapitalization—especially in brick-and-mortar businesses that sell or make something, rather than service-based businesses. The rule of thumb is that you should have access to money equal to your first year's anticipated profits, plus start-up expenses. (Note that this is not the same as having the money on hand—see the discussion on lines of credit, below.) For instance, if your annual rent, salaries, and equipment will cost $50,000 and you expect $25,000 worth of profit in your first year, you should have access to $75,000 worth of financing.

You need to decide what sort of financing you will need. Small business loans have both advantages and disadvantages. They can provide critical start-up credit, but in order to obtain one, your personal credit will need to be good, and you will, of course, have to pay them off with interest. In general, the more you and your partners put into the business yourselves, the more credit lenders will be willing to extend to you.

Equity can come from your own personal investment, either in cash or an equity loan on your home. You may also want to consider bringing on partners—at least limited financial partners—as a way to cover start-up costs.

It is also worth considering obtaining a line of credit instead of a loan. A loan is taken out all at once, but with a line of credit, you draw on the money as you need it. This both saves you interest payments and means that you have the money you need when you need it. Taking out too large of a loan can be worse than having no money at all! It just sits there collecting interest—or, worse, is spent on something utterly un-necessary—and then is not around when you need it most.

The first five years are the hardest for any business venture; your venture has about double the usual chance of closing in this time (1 out of 6, rather than 1 out of 12). You will probably have to tighten your belt at home, as well as work long hours and keep careful track of your business expenses. Be careful with your money. Do not take unnecessary risks, play it conservatively, and always keep some capital in reserve for emergencies. The hardest part of a new business, of course, is the learning curve of figuring out what, exactly, you need to do to make a profit, and so the best advice is to have plenty of savings—or a job to provide income—while you learn the ropes.

One thing you should not do is count on venture capitalists or "angel investors," that is, businesspeople who make a living investing on other businesses in the hopes that their equity in the company will increase in value. Venture capitalists have gotten something of a reputation as indiscriminate spendthrifts due to some poor choices made during the dot-com boom of the late 1990s, but the fact is that most do not take risks on unproven products. Rather, they are attracted to young companies that have the potential to become regional or national powerhouses and give better-than-average returns. Nor are venture capitalists endless sources of money; rather, they are savvy businesspeople who are usually attracted to companies that have already experienced a measure of success. Therefore, it is better to rely on your own resources until you have proven your business will work.

Bookkeeping 101

The principles of double-entry bookkeeping have not changed much since its invention in the fifteenth century: one column records debits, and one records credits. The trick is *doing* it. As a small business owner, you need to be disciplined and meticulous at recording your finances. Thankfully, today there is software available that can do everything from tracking payables and receivables to running checks and generating reports.

Honestly ask yourself if you are the sort of person who does a good job keeping track of finances. If you are not, outsource to a bookkeeping company or hire someone to come in once or twice a week to enter invoices and generate checks for you. Also remember that if you have employees or even freelancers, you will have to file tax forms for them at the end of the year.

Another good idea is to have an accountant for your business to handle advice and taxes (federal, state, local, sales tax, etc.). In fact, consulting with a certified public accountant is a good idea in general, since they are usually aware of laws and rules that you have never even heard of.

Finally, keep your personal and business accounting separate. If your business ever gets audited, the first thing the IRS looks for is personal expenses disguised as business expenses. A good accountant can help you to know what are legitimate business expenses. Everything you take from the business account, such as payroll and reimbursement, must be recorded and classified.

Being an Employer

Know your situation regarding employees. To begin with, if you have any employees, you will need an Employer Identification Number (EIN), also sometimes called a Federal Tax Identification Number. Getting an EIN is simple: You can fill out IRS form SS-4, or complete the process online at http://www.irs.gov.

Having employees carries other responsibilities and legalities with it. To begin with, you will need to pay payroll taxes (otherwise known as "withholding") to cover income tax, unemployment insurance, Social Security, and Medicare, as well as file W-2 and W-4 forms with the government. You will also be required to pay worker's compensation insurance, and will probably also want to find medical insurance. You are also required to abide by your state's nondiscrimination laws. Most states require you to post nondiscrimination and compensation notices in a public area.

Many employers are tempted to unofficially hire workers "off the books." This can have advantages, but can also mean entering a legal gray area. (Note, however, this is different from hiring freelancers, a temp employed by another company, or having a self-employed professional such as an accountant or bookkeeper come in occasionally to provide a service.) It is one thing to hire the neighbor's teenage son on a one-time basis to help you move some boxes, but quite another to have full-time workers working on a cash-and-carry basis. Regular wages must be noted in the accounts, and gaps may be questioned in the event of an audit. If the workers are injured on the job, you are not covered by worker's comp, and are thus vulnerable to lawsuits. If the workers you hired are not legal residents, you can also be liable for civil and criminal penalties. In general, it is best to keep your employees as above-board as possible.

Building a Business

Good business practices are essential to success. First off, do not overextend yourself. Be honest about what you can do and in what time frame. Secondly, be a responsible business owner. In general, if there is a problem, it is best to explain matters honestly to your clients than to leave them without word and wondering. In the former case, there is at least the possibility of salvaging your reputation and credibility.

Most business is still built by personal contacts and word of mouth. It is for this reason that maintaining your list of contacts is an essential practice. Even if a particular contact may not be useful at a particular moment, a future opportunity may present itself—or you may be able to send someone else to them. Networking, in other words, is as important when you are the boss as when you are looking for a job yourself. As the owner of a company, having a network means getting services on better terms, knowing where to go if you need help with a particular problem, or simply being in the right place at the right time to exploit an opportunity. Join professional organizations, the local Chamber of Commerce, clubs and community organizations, and learn to play golf. And remember—never burn a bridge.

Advertising is another way to build a business. Planning an ad campaign is not as difficult as you might think: You probably already know your media market and business community. The trick is applying it. Again, go with your instincts. If you never look twice at your local weekly, other people probably do not, either. If you are in a high-tourist area, though, local tourist maps might be a good way to leverage your marketing dollar. Ask other people in your area or market who have businesses similar to your own. Depending on your focus, you might want to consider everything from AM radio or local TV networks, to national trade publications, to hiring a PR firm for an all-out blitz. By thinking about these questions, you can spend your advertising dollars most effectively.

Nor should you underestimate the power of using the Internet to build your business. It is a very powerful tool for small businesses, potentially reaching vast numbers of people for relatively little outlay of money. Launching a Web site has become the modern equivalent of hanging out your shingle. Even if you are primarily a brick-and-mortar business, a Web presence can still be an invaluable tool—your store or offices will show up on Google searches, plus customers can find directions to visit you in person. Furthermore, the Internet offers the small-business owner many useful tools. Print and design services, order fulfillment, credit card processing, and networking—both personal and in terms of linking to other sites—are all available online. Web advertising can be useful, too, either by advertising on specialty sites that appeal to your audience, or by using services such as Google AdWords.

Amateurish print ads, TV commercials, and Web sites do not speak well of your business. Good media should be well-designed, well-edited, and well-put together. It need not, however, be expensive. Shop around and, again, use your network.

Flexibility is also important. "In general, a business must adapt to changing conditions, find new customers and find new products or services that customers need when the demand for their older products or services diminishes," says James Peck, a Long Island, New York, entrepreneur. In other words, if your original plan is not working out, or if demand falls, see if you can parlay your experience, skills, and physical plant into meeting other needs. People are not the only ones who can change their path in life; organizations can, too.

A Final Word

In business, as in other areas of life, the advice of more experienced people is essential. "I think it really takes three businesses until you know what you're doing," Drew Curtis confides. "I sure didn't know what I was doing the first time." Listen to what others have to say, no matter whether it is about your Web site or your business plan. One possible solution is seeking out a mentor, someone who has previously launched a successful venture in this field. In any case, before taking any step, ask as many people as many questions as you can. Good advice is invaluable.

Further Resources

American Independent Business Alliance
http://www.amiba.net

American Small Business League
http://www.asbl.com

IRS Small Business and Self-Employed One-Stop Resource
http://www.irs.gov/businesses/small/index.html

The Riley Guide: Steps in Starting Your Own Business
http://www.rileyguide.com/steps.html

Small Business Administration
http://www.sba.gov

Appendix B

Outfitting Yourself for Career Success

As you contemplate a career shift, the first component is to assess your interests. You need to figure out what makes you tick, since there is a far greater chance that you will enjoy and succeed in a career that taps into your passions, inclinations, natural abilities, and training. If you have a general idea of what your interests are, you at least know in which direction you want to travel. You may know you want to simply switch from one sort of nursing to another, or change your life entirely and pursue a dream you have always held. In this case, you can use a specific volume of The Field Guides to Finding a New Career to discover which position to target. If you are unsure of the direction you want to take, well, then the entire scope of the series is open to you! Browse through to see what appeals to you, and see if it matches with your experience and abilities.

The next step you should take is to make a list—do it once in writing—of the skills you have used in a position of responsibility that transfer to the field you are entering. People in charge of interviewing and hiring may well understand that the skills they are looking for in a new hire are used in other fields, but you must spell it out. Most job descriptions are partly a list of skills. Map your experience into that, and very early in your contacts with a prospective employer explicitly address how you acquired your relevant skills. Pick a relatively unimportant aspect of the job to be your ready answer for where you would look forward to learning within the organization, if this seems essentially correct. When you transfer into a field, softly acknowledge a weakness while relating your readiness to learn, but never lose sight of the value you offer both in your abilities and in the freshness of your perspective.

Energy and Experience

The second component in career-switching success is energy. When Jim Fulmer was 61, he found himself forced to close his piano-repair business. However, he was able to parlay his knowledge of music, pianos, and the musical instruments industry into another job as a sales representative for a large piano manufacturer, and quickly built up a clientele of musical-instrument retailers throughout the East Coast. Fulmer's experience highlights another essential lesson for career-changers: There are plenty of opportunities out there, but jobs will not come to you—especially the career-oriented, well-paying ones. You have to seek them out.

Jim Fulmer's case also illustrates another important point: Former training and experience can be a key to success. "Anyone who has to make a career change in any stage of life has to look at what skills they have acquired but may not be aware of," he says. After all, people can more easily change into careers similar to the ones they are leaving. Training and experience also let you enter with a greater level of seniority, provided you have the other necessary qualifications. For instance, a nurse who is already experienced with administering drugs and their benefits and drawbacks, and who is also graced with the personality and charisma to work with the public, can become a pharmaceutical company sales representative.

Unlock Your Network

The next step toward unlocking the perfect job is networking. The term may be overused, but the idea is as old as civilization. More than other animals, humans need one another. With the Internet and telephone, never in history has it been easier to form (or revive) these essential links. One does not have to gird oneself and attend reunion-type events (though for many this is a fine tactic)—but keep open to opportunities to meet people who may be friendly to you in your field. Ben Franklin understood the principle well—*Poor Richard's Almanac* is something of a treatise on the importance of cultivating what Franklin called "friendships" with benefactors. So follow in the steps of the founding fathers and make friends to get ahead. Remember: helping others feels good; it's often the receiving that gets a little tricky. If you know someone particularly well-connected in your field, consider tapping one or two less important connections first so that you make the most of the important one. As you proceed, keep your strengths foremost in your mind because the glue of commerce is mutual interest.

Eighty percent of job openings are *never advertised*, and, according to the U.S. Bureau of Labor statistics, more than half of all employees landed their jobs through networking. Using your personal contacts is far more efficient and effective than trusting your résumé to the Web. On the Web, an employer needs to sort through tens of thousands—or millions—of résumés. When you direct your application to one potential employer, you are directing your inquiry to one person who already knows you. The personal touch is everything: Human beings are social animals, programmed to "read" body language; we are naturally inclined to trust those we meet in person, or who our friends and coworkers have recommended. While Web sites can be useful (for looking through help-wanted ads, for instance), expecting employers to pick you out of the slush pile is as effective as throwing your résumé into a black hole.

Do not send your résumé out just to make yourself feel like you're doing something. The proper way to go about things is to employ discipline and order, and then to apply your charm. Begin your networking efforts by making a list of people you can talk to: colleagues, coworkers, and supervisors, people you have had working relationship with, people from church, athletic teams, political organizations, or other community groups, friends, and relatives. You can expand your networking opportunities by following the suggestions in each chapter of the volumes. Your goal here is not so much to land a job as to expand your possibilities and knowledge: Though the people on your list may not be in the position to help you themselves, they might know someone who is. Meeting with them might also help you understand traits that matter and skills that are valued in the field in which you are interested. Even if the person is a potential employer, it is best to phrase your request as if you were seeking information: "You might not be able to help me, but do you know someone I could talk to who could tell me more about what it is like to work in this field?" Being hungry gives one impression, being desperate quite another.

Keep in mind that networking is a two-way street. If you meet someone who has an opening that is not right for you, but you could recommend someone else, you have just added to your list two people who will be favorably disposed toward you in the future. Also, bear in mind that *you* can help people in *your* old field, thus adding to your own contacts list.

Networking is especially important to the self-employed or those who start their own businesses. Many people in this situation begin because they either recognize a potential market in a field that they are familiar with, or because full-time employment in this industry is no longer a possibility. Already being well-established in a field can help, but so can asking connections for potential work and generally making it known that you are ready, willing, and able to work. Working your professional connections, in many cases, is the *only* way to establish yourself. A freelancer's network, in many cases, is like a spider's web. The spider casts out many strands, since he or she never knows which one might land the next meal.

Dial-Up Help

In general, it is better to call contacts directly than to e-mail them. E-mails are easy for busy people to ignore or overlook, even if they do not mean to. Explain your situation as briefly as possible (see the discussion of the "elevator speech"), and ask if you could meet briefly, either at their office or at a neutral place such as a café. (Be sure that you pay the bill in such a situation—it is a way of showing you appreciate their time and effort.) If you get someone's voicemail, give your "elevator speech" and then say you will call back in a few days to follow up—and then do so. If you reach your contact directly and they are too busy to speak or meet with you, make a definite appointment to call back at a later date. Be persistent, but not annoying.

Once you have arranged a meeting, prep yourself. Look at industry publications both in print and online, as well as news reports (here, GoogleNews, which lets you search through online news reports, can be very handy). Having up-to-date information on industry trends shows that you are dedicated, knowledgeable, and focused. Having specific questions on employers and requests for suggestions will set you apart from the rest of the job-hunting pack. Knowing the score—for instance, asking about the value of one sort of certification instead of another—pegs you as an "insider," rather than a dilettante, someone whose name is worth remembering and passing along to a potential employer.

Finally, set the right mood. Here, a little self-hypnosis goes a long way: Look at yourself in the mirror, and tell yourself that you are an enthusiastic, committed professional. Mood affects confidence and performance. Discipline your mind so you keep your perspective and self-respect. Nobody wants to hire someone who comes across as insincere, tells a sob story, or is still in the doldrums of having lost their previous job. At the end of any networking meeting, ask for someone else who might be able to help you in your journey to finding a position in this field, either with information or a potential job opening.

Get a Lift

When you meet with a contact in person (as well as when you run into anyone by chance who may be able to help you), you need an "elevator speech" (so-named because it should be short enough to be delivered during an elevator ride from a ground level to a high floor). This is a summary in which, in less than two minutes, you give them a clear impression of who you are, where you come from, your experience and goals, and why you are on the path you are on. The motto above Plato's Academy holds true: Know Thyself (this is where our Career Compasses and guides will help you). A long and rambling "elevator story" will get you nowhere. Furthermore, be positive: Neither a sad-sack story nor a tirade explaining how everything that went wrong in your old job is someone else's fault will get you anywhere. However, an honest explanation of a less-than-fortunate circumstance, such as a decline in business forcing an office closure, needing to change residence to a place where you are not qualified to work in order to further your spouse's career, or needing to work fewer hours in order to care for an ailing family member, is only honest.

An elevator speech should show 1) you know the business involved; 2) you know the company; 3) you are qualified (here, try to relate your education and work experience to the new situation); and 4) you are goal-oriented, dependable, and hardworking. Striking a balance is important; you want to sound eager, but not overeager. You also want to show a steady work experience, but not that you have been so narrowly focused that you cannot adjust. Most important is emphasizing what you can do for the company. You will be surprised how much information you can include in two minutes. Practice this speech in front of a mirror until you have the key points down perfectly. It should sound natural, and you should come across as friendly, confident, and assertive. Finally, remember eye contact! Good eye contact needs to be part of your presentation, as well as your everyday approach when meeting potential employers and leads.

Get Your Résumé Ready

Everyone knows what a résumé is, but how many of us have really thought about how to put one together? Perhaps no single part of the job search is subject to more anxiety—or myths and misunderstandings— than this 8 ½-by-11-inch sheet of paper.

On the one hand, it is perfectly all right for someone—especially in certain careers, such as academia—to have a résumé that is more than one page. On the other hand, you do not need to tell a future employer *everything*. Trim things down to the most relevant; for a 40-year-old to mention an internship from two decades ago is superfluous. Likewise, do not include irrelevant jobs, lest you seem like a professional career-changer.

Tailor your descriptions of your former employment to the particular position you are seeking. This is not to say you should lie, but do make your experience more appealing. If the job you're looking for involves supervising other people, say if you have done this in the past; if it involves specific knowledge or capabilities, mention that you possess these qualities. In general, try to make your past experience seem similar to what you are seeking.

The standard advice is to put your Job Objective at the heading of the résumé. An alternative to this is a Professional Summary, which some recruiters and employers prefer. The difference is that a Job Objective mentions the position you are seeking, whereas a Professional Summary mentions your background (e.g. "Objective: To find a position as a sales representative in agribusiness machinery" versus "Experienced sales representative; strengths include background in agribusiness, as well as building team dynamics and market expansion"). Of course, it is easy to come up with two or three versions of the same document for different audiences.

The body of the résumé of an experienced worker varies a lot more than it does at the beginning of your career. You need not put your education or your job experience first; rather, your résumé should emphasize your strengths. If you have a master's degree in a related field, that might want to go before your unrelated job experience. Conversely, if too much education will harm you, you might want to bury that under the section on professional presentations you have given that show how good you are at communicating. If you are currently enrolled in a course or other professional development, be sure to note this (as well as your date of expected graduation). A résumé is a study of blurs, highlights, and jewels. You blur everything you must in order to fit the description of your experience to the job posting. You highlight what is relevant from each and any of your positions worth mentioning. The jewels are the little headers and such—craft them, since they are what is seen first.

You may also want to include professional organizations, work-related achievements, and special abilities, such as your fluency in a foreign language. Also mention your computer software qualifications and capabilities, especially if you are looking for work in a technological field or if you are an older job-seeker who might be perceived as behind the technology curve. Including your interests or family information might or might not be a good idea—no one really cares about your bridge club, and in fact they might worry that your marathon training might take away from your work commitments, but, on the other hand, mentioning your golf handicap or three children might be a good idea if your potential employer is an avid golfer or is a family woman herself.

You can either include your references or simply note, "References available upon request." However, be sure to ask your references' permission to use their names and alert them to the fact that they may be contacted before you include them on your résumé! Be sure to include name, organization, phone number, and e-mail address for each contact.

Today, word processors make it easy to format your résumé. However, beware of prepackaged résumé "wizards"—they do not make you stand out in the crowd. Feel free to strike out on your own, but remember the most important thing in formatting a résumé is consistency. Unless you have a background in typography, do not get too fancy. Finally, be sure to have someone (or several people!) read your résumé over for you.

For more information on résumé writing, check out Web sites such as http://www.résumé.monster.com.

Craft Your Cover Letter

It is appropriate to include a cover letter with your résumé. A cover letter lets you convey extra information about yourself that does not fit or is not always appropriate in your résumé, such as why you are no longer working in your original field of employment. You can and should also mention the name of anyone who referred you to the job. You can go into some detail about the reason you are a great match, given the job description. Also address any questions that might be raised in the potential employer's mind (for instance, a gap in employment). Do not, however, ramble on. Your cover letter should stay focused on your goal: To offer a strong, positive impression of yourself and persuade the hiring manager that you are worth an interview. Your cover letter gives you a chance to stand out from the other applicants and sell yourself. In fact, according to a CareerBuilder.com survey, 23 percent of hiring managers say a candidate's ability to relate his or her experience to the job at hand is a top hiring consideration.

Even if you are not a great writer, you can still craft a positive yet concise cover letter in three paragraphs: An introduction containing the specifics of the job you are applying for; a summary of why you are a good fit for the position and what you can do for the company; and a closing with a request for an interview, contact information, and thanks. Remember to vary the structure and tone of your cover letter—do not begin every sentence with "I."

Ace Your Interview

In truth, your interview begins well before you arrive. Be sure to have read up well on the company and its industry. Use Web sites and magazines—http://www.hoovers.com offers free basic business information, and trade magazines deliver both information and a feel for the industries they cover. Also, do not neglect talking to people in your circle who might know about trends in the field. Leave enough time to digest the information so that you can give some independent thought to the company's history and prospects. You don't need to be an expert when you arrive to be interviewed; but you should be comfortable. The most important element of all is to be poised and relaxed during the interview itself. Preparation and practice can help a lot.

Be sure to develop well-thought-through answers to the following, typical interview openers and standard questions.

☞ Tell me about yourself. (Do not complain about how unsatisfied you were in your former career, but give a brief summary of your applicable background and interest in the particular job area.) If there is a basis to it, emphasize how much you love to work and how you are a team player.

☞ Why do you want this job? (Speak from the brain, and the heart—of course you want the money, but say a little here about what you find interesting about the field and the company's role in it.)

☞ What makes you a good hire? (Remember here to connect the company's needs and your skill set. Ultimately, your selling points probably come down to one thing: you will make your employer money. You want the prospective hirer to see that your skills are valuable not to the world in general but to this specific company's bottom line. What can you do for them?)

☞ What led you to leave your last job? (If you were fired, still try to say something positive, such as, "The business went through a challenging time, and some of the junior marketing people were let go.")

Practice answering these and other questions, and try to be genuinely positive about yourself, and patient with the process. Be secure but not cocky; don't be shy about forcing the focus now and then on positive contributions you have made in your working life—just be specific. As with the elevator speech, practice in front of the mirror.

A couple pleasantries are as natural a way as any to start the actual interview, but observe the interviewer closely for any cues to fall silent and formally begin. Answer directly; when in doubt, finish your phrase and look to the interviewer. Without taking command, you can always ask, "Is there more you would like to know?" Your attentiveness will convey respect. Let your personality show too—a positive attitude and a grounded sense of your abilities will go a long way to getting you considered. During the interview, keep your cell phone off and do not look at your watch. Toward the end of your meeting, you may be asked whether you have any questions. It is a good idea to have one or two in mind. A few examples follow:

☞ "What makes your company special in the field?"
☞ "What do you consider the hardest part of this position?"
☞ "Where are your greatest opportunities for growth?"
☞ "Do you know when you might need anything further from me?"

Leave discussion of terms for future conversations. Make a cordial, smooth exit.

Remember to Follow Up

Send a thank-you note. Employers surveyed by CareerBuilder.com in 2005 said it matters. About 15 percent said they would not hire someone who did not follow up with a thanks. And almost 33 percent would think less of a candidate. The form of the note does not much matter—if you know a manager's preference, use it. Otherwise, just be sure to follow up.

Winning an Offer

A job offer can feel like the culmination of a long and difficult struggle. So naturally, when you hear them, you may be tempted to jump at the offer. Don't. Once an employer wants you, he or she will usually give you a chance to consider the offer. This is the time to discuss terms of employment, such as vacation, overtime, and benefits. A little effort now can be well worth it in the future. Be sure to do a check of prevailing salaries for your field and area before signing on. Web sites for this include Payscale.com, Salary.com, and Salaryexpert.com. If you are thinking about asking for better or different terms from what the prospective employer offered, rest assured—that's how business gets done; and it may just burnish the positive impression you have already made.

Index